# MAKING OUT IN INDONESIAN

**TUTTLE** Publishing

Tokyo | Rutland, Vermont | Singapore

# Contents

# Introduction

So someone told you that Indonesian was an "easy language". You diligently learned the phrases at the back of your guidebook. You bought a home-learning course and trudged through its units—and yes, Indonesian grammar did seem pretty straightforward. You practiced earnestly on the staff in the hotel in Bali. They smiled politely and said that you were very **pintar** (clever). Everything seemed to be going so well—that is, until you attempted to have anything more than the most rudimentary interaction in Indonesian out on the street, or to eavesdrop on two locals in conversation.

The trouble is that Indonesian as it is actually used day-to-day is a very different thing from the language that is usually laid out in textbooks and phrasebooks. This can make life frustrating for would-be learners, so the aim of this book is to give you an introduction to the practical version of real spoken Indonesian. It won't make you into an overnight linguistic virtuoso (you'll need half a lifetime of immersion to get to that stage) or place you at the cutting edge of modern youth-speak (you'd need a permanent social media connection and the mental processing power of a supercomputer to keep up with *that* aspect of the language). However, if you're already in the process of learning Indonesian it will help jumpstart you beyond the clunky formality stage, and if you're just starting out it'll give you a head start towards sounding a little less like a robot when you ask directions, order lunch, or haggle in the market! And the great news is that once you break away from the starchy syntax of formal Indonesian, it turns out to be a fabulously fun language, packing maximum expressiveness into very few words.

Languages, of course, are living things, closely bound up with the cultures of the people who speak them, so we've also peppered this book with some little tidbits to help you make sense of the wonderfully exciting country and people to which this language belongs.

## INTRODUCING INDONESIAN

What exactly is Indonesian? The language refers to itself as **Bahasa Indonesia**. This simply means "Indonesian Language"—so don't make the classic beginner's error of asking, "Do you speak Bahasa?" The natural response to that would be: "Umm… *which* Bahasa?"

You'll sometimes hear people say that Indonesian is some kind of "made-up language", a Southeast Asian answer to Esperanto, invented by the nationalist movement in the early twentieth century. But this idea is based on a misunderstanding. Indonesian nationalists, campaigning for independence from Holland, did indeed invent a new name for the language (**Bahasa Indonesia**), but not the language itself. That had been around for millennia—it just used to be called "Malay".

Indonesia is home to literally hundreds of other distinct languages and regional dialects, but these days almost everyone in this quarter-billion-strong population also speaks Indonesian. Apart from very remote rural areas, virtually everyone under the age of 50 is at least fluent in Indonesian, and in some places it has taken over from regional dialects as a first language.

## BAHASA MELAYU

The language originally known as Malay has long been the lingua franca of Southeast Asia, good to get you by in harbor towns everywhere from southern Thailand to the borders of Papua New Guinea. Indonesian is the modern incarnation of Malay, but there are also other versions of the language spoken in Malaysia, Singapore and Brunei. The "Bahasa Melayu" of those neighboring countries is still very closely related to Indonesian, and fluent speakers of one can generally understand and make themselves understood in the other. But the languages are different enough that Malaysian movies and TV shows usually get dubbed or subtitled when they're imported to Indonesia, and vice versa. A case in point: if you wanted to ask "Do you speak Indonesian?" in Bahasa Melayu you'd probably say **Boléh cakap Bahasa Indonesia?** Now, Indonesian-speakers would definitely understand those words, but they wouldn't ask the question using these words—their version would be something like **Bisa Bahasa Indonesia?**

## RULES OF THE GAME

A first glance at the Indonesian rule book is a refreshing experience for any English-speaker who's previously struggled to learn another European language, still less something like Hebrew or Arabic. It all seems so straight-forward! Tenses, when they're used at all, are formed with marker words, leaving the core verbs unchanged. Pronouns don't go shapeshifting—"he", "him" and "his" are all covered by a single word. There's no gender, and to all intents and purposes no plurals. Articles, definite and indefinite, don't exist (well, rough equivalents for "a" and "the" actually do exist, but you don't need to worry about them in the sort of Indonesian you're learning here). And individual words are entirely unaffected by their neighbors in any given sentence—verbs remain blissfully unbothered by a change in the preceding pronoun.

But don't get too excited! Because once you get beyond the basics you'll quickly discover that Indonesian has other complications all of its own…

## BUILDING BLOCKS

The main building blocks of Indonesian are root words from which verbs, nouns and adjectives can be built. Let's take as an example the word **bicara**, "speak".

### NEW BEGINNINGS

To create the full form of a verb you add one of two prefixes—**ber** or **me** (the **ber** prefix sometimes becomes **bel** or **be**, and the **me** prefix sometimes needs to become **mem**, **meng** or occasionally **meny**, depending on the root it's attaching to). **Bicara** takes the **ber** prefix, becoming **berbicara** = "to speak".

To create the most obviously related noun from a root, you typically add the suffix **an**. So **bicaraan** is... yes, you've guessed it: "conversation".

And the equivalent of sticking "-er" on the end of an English verb is to place the **pe** prefix (which sometimes has to become **pem** or **pel**, depending on the root) up front. So **pembicara** is "speaker".

So far, so simple, but unfortunately, things get murkier from hereon in, with a series of other prefixes, suffixes, and prefix-suffix combos which have more abstract effects on the root. **Membicarakan** means "to discuss something". **Pembicaraan** is "discussion".

## PASSIVELY SPEAKING

Then there's the Indonesians' love of that floppy, flaccid thing that English-language journalists are always taught to avoid—the passive voice. It's used far more often in Indonesian than in English, and it's usually formed with the prefix **di**, or, less frequently, with the prefix **ter** (which, confusingly, is also used to make superlatives such as **terbesar**, "the biggest"). So **dibicarakan** means "to be discussed". **Tertipu** means "tricked", as in **aku tertipu**, "I was tricked", from **tipu**, "trick".

## GETTING ABSTRACT

Then there's the **ke-an** prefix-suffix combo. Usually this is used to make an abstract noun from a root word or a related noun—so **keuangan** means "finance", from **uang** which means "money". Unfortunately, however, the **ke-an** combo also does other things. It can create a particularly abstract sort of adjective, such as **kehujanan** (from **hujan**, "rain") which means "the soggy state you find yourself in if you get caught out in the rain without an umbrella"—or something to that effect, anyway. **Ke-an** can also be used to create new verbs with specialized meanings out of old verbs—for example **ketiduran**, "to fall asleep", from **tidur**, "to sleep". And as for how you tell which function a particular **ke-an** combo is serving—unfortunately you just have to develop a feel for it, which only comes with a fairly high level of Indonesian proficiency. Either that, or simply memorize each instance, one by one.

This tendency to build up new words by adding bits and pieces to the beginnings and endings of simple root words creates some monstrous multisyllabic mouthfuls in formal Indonesian. Just take a look at any book or newspaper and you'll find them—more like lateral thinking puzzles than normal words (or, a bit like German).

Did someone tell you that Indonesian was "an easy language"?

But fear not. When it comes to the kind of everyday spoken Indonesian that we'll be covering in this book, and that is often used by Indonesians when conversing casually, you can dispense with a lot of this stuff.

## SPEAKING SIMPLY

If you do want to truly master the language you will eventually need to get to grips with all the arcane details. But when you're out and about on the streets, actually speaking to real people, you can usually forget them, because the very best thing about informal Indonesian is that, thanks to its long history as a regional lingua franca, it puts a high value on economy. And most people don't care at all for the highfalutin formal language with all its fancy prefixes and suffixes.

Let's go back to our root word, **bicara**, to illustrate.

Most traditional phrasebooks will tell you that if you want to ask, "Do you speak Indonesian?" you'll need to say **Bisakah anda berbicara Bahasa Indonesia?** (Spot the **bicara** root in there somewhere?) But when Indonesians actually ask that question in real life they don't bother with all that stuff; they'll just say **Bisa bicara Bahasa Indonesia?** (literally "Can speak Indonesian?"), or even just **Bisa Bahasa Indonesia?** (literally "Can Indonesian?") After all, why bother with five words when three will do?

## PRONUNCIATION

Helpfully, Indonesian is written in the same Roman alphabet that we use for English. Even more helpfully, its spelling system is supremely logical and consistent— unlike English! If you see an Indonesian word written down, you generally know exactly how to say it. And there's yet more good news. Although it usually takes long exposure to the spoken language before you can begin to convincingly replicate the distinctive accent and intonation of native Indonesian speakers, when it comes to the basic pronunciation there's very little that would baffle an English speaker.

## VOWELS

a       as in p**a**r

i       a mid-length vowel, halfway between h**i**t and h**ea**t

o       as in d**o**g

u       a mid-length vowel, halfway between c**u**t and c**oo**t

e       this is Indonesian's only inconsistent letter. Nine times out of ten an **e** is pronounced as the very short, neutral vowel technically known as a "schwa", as in the final syllable of bot**tle**. Occasionally, however, it is pronounced as in b**e**t. There's no differentiation between these two pronunciations in the normal Indonesian writing system, but to help you out here we'll use a regular "e" to represent the short "schwa" sound and an accented "é" for the other, longer kind of "e".

ai, au,  when two vowels appear side by side in

ia       Indonesian they create what is technically known in English as a "diphthong"—in other words, the two distinct vowel sounds run together, creating a long vowel sound with a slight bend in the middle. The diphthong in **air** ("water"—yes, really!) is pronounced as in h**ire**; **mau** ("want) as in c**ow**; **dia** ("he/she") as in med**ia**.

## CONSONANTS

b       as in **b**ig

c       as in **ch**ild—take careful note of this one: an Indonesian **c** is always pronounced as an English "ch" (never as "s" or "k")

d       as in **d**ig

| | |
|---|---|
| **f** | as in **f**ig—**f** doesn't actually occur naturally in Indonesian, and it usually only appears in words that originated from Arabic. In informal speech **f** and **p** (which is a native Indonesian sound) are sometimes interchangeable, especially if the **f** comes at the start of the word. Some people say **fikir**, others say **pikir**; both mean "to think". |
| **g** | as in **g**o—always a hard "g" |
| **h** | as in **h**it—an "h" at the end of a word like **boléh** ("may") should be pronounced, which a little extra push of breath. On the other hand, where **h** appears between two vowels, as in **lihat** ("to see"), it tends to vanish in casual speech, becoming **liat**. |
| **j** | as in **j**ack |
| **k** | as in **k**ick |
| **l** | as in **l**ike |
| **m** | as in **m**at |
| **n** | as in **n**ot |
| **p** | as in **p**en |
| **s** | as in **s**at |
| **t** | as in **t**oy |
| **v** | **v** only appears in loanwords from other languages, and Indonesians tend to pronounce it between an English **f** and a **v** |
| **w** | as in **w**ood |
| **y** | as in **y**et |
| **z** | as in **z**ebra |

And a couple of slightly trickier ones…

| | |
|---|---|
| **r** | **r** is rolled as in Spanish—if you can't roll your **r**, don't worry; there are actually some Indonesians |

who can't manage it either. They tend to deal with the problem by giving the letter a gentle rasp, a bit like in the French pronunciation of "Paris". Otherwise, just leave it like a soft English **r**, and you'll still be understood.

**ng**    this is the one Indonesian sound that foreigners tend to get freaked out by, but actually it's not at all alien to English speakers. We use it every time we say si**ng**, sa**ng**, or su**ng**. Slightly more challenging is the fact that it sometimes turns up at the start of an Indonesian word—especially in the informal version of the language, with words such as **ngomong** (slang for "to speak"). The challenge here is more that English speakers aren't used to using this sound in this position, rather than that they can't make it at all. The important thing to remember is that when you encounter the **ng** followed immediately by a second **g**—as in **tinggal** ("stay")—you need to pronounce both letters clearly: **ting-gal**.

**ny**    rolled together as in ca**ny**on

**sy**    this only appears in Arabic loanwords, and it's the best-guess Indonesian approximation of the English **sh** sound, as in **sh**ake. The closest most Indonesians can get is indeed **s** rolled into **y**, but you can also pronounce it as **sh**.

**kh**    another feature of Arabic loanwords, it's pronounced like a softer version of the rasping **ch** in the proper Scottish pronunciation of lo**ch**, or the guttural French **r** in Pa**r**is

Ending words with **k** and **t**

> when the letters **k** and **t** appear at the end of an
> Indonesian word—as in **tidak** ("no") and **lihat**
> ("see") they almost vanish—but not quite.
> Technically, they are "unaspirated": where in
> English they would come with a final little push of
> breath, in Indonesian they are cut off just before
> that point, so that your tongue doesn't leave your
> teeth/roof of your mouth at the end of the word.
> Try it! You'll see what we mean!

## REAL SPOKEN INDONESIAN

As we've already pointed out, the single most notable
feature of informal, everyday Indonesian is its economy.
Extraneous words get stripped out and thrown away,
reducing what would be a two-line sentence in a standard
phrasebook to just a couple of words. Pronouns, in
particular, tend to get dropped, and it's sometimes
possible to have an entire conversation without using the
words "I" or "you" (this is actually quite helpful, as you'd
often have to choose an Indonesian form of these
particular pronouns, depending on the circumstances—an
issue we'll cover later on).

But just because a language is being spoken informally,
doesn't mean that grammar rules no longer apply. This
book doesn't aim to provide a detailed introduction to
Indonesian grammar, but where a particularly important
rule or convention applies to a phrase, we'll provide a
useful explanation.

Just as in spoken English, the words that Indonesian speakers use are often not those that you would find if you delved into a dictionary. In some cases the word usually used in casual conversation bears absolutely no resemblance to its formal counterpart—we've already met **bicara**, the dictionary word for "speak", and its radically different informal equivalent **ngomong** (or **omong** for short).

In other cases, however, the original formal word simply gets a modification or an abbreviation. A number of commonly used Indonesian words lose their initial letter in everyday use, not least **sudah**, "already", both a tense marker and important for asking and answering questions. In general speech it's usually shortened to **udah**. There are also times when the pronunciation of a word shifts slightly from the "correct" version. It's common for a final-syllable **a** to get turned into an **e** (the short, schwa version) in informal conversation. So **malas** ("lazy") becomes **males**, and **pintar** ("clever") becomes **pinter**. We use the commonest of these popular modifications throughout this book, to help give your Indonesian an authentic edge. But you do still need to know the "correct" way to say things, so wherever a slang term first appears, we'll also give you a "Slang Alert" and let you know the more formal version of the word.

## SPEAKING SOCIALLY

At its leading edge, informal everyday Indonesian turns into a terrifyingly incomprehensible patois, usually known as **Bahasa Gaul**, literally "social language", but perhaps better thought of as "youth-speak". Teenagers and street kids in the big cities have always had their own, fast-talking, slang-laden forms of speech, but in recent decades the inventiveness and impenetrability of **Bahasa Gaul** has shifted to an entirely new level, given a rocket-fuel boost by social media. Not only does it feature extreme abbreviations and wildly inventive slang; it sometimes even has its own distinct grammar rules. And, unsurprisingly, it is fragmented into various versions, unique to particular cities or subcultures.

The most striking thing about twenty-first-century **Bahasa Gaul** is the speed at which it changes, new words and constructions seemingly sprouting with every fresh Instagram post. For this reason we haven't tried to turn this book into a crash course in **Bahasa Gaul**. It would've been out of date before we'd even finished writing it, and you'd end up sounding like a wannabe trying to talk like a 1970s New Yorker in twenty-first-century Los Angeles!

Instead, this book focuses on the more general everyday language, spoken by everyone from one end of Indonesia to the other. Some **Bahasa Gaul** innovations—those shifts from **a** to **e** at the end of some words, for example—do become so common that they cross over into the mainstream. But we've made sure to include only those that would be familiar to everyone and that have been around long enough to be more than a passing affectation. After all, you might want to sound more natural when you're speaking Indonesian, but you would still need to be understood by everyone, from teenage hipsters to kindly grandmas!

# 1

# Nuts and Bolts

## HOW THE LANGUAGE WORKS

In this section we'll give you an introduction to the essential features of the sentence structure in colloquial Indonesian, to help you make sense of how the phrases that appear in the rest of this book are actually put together. That way you won't simply be reciting, parrot-fashion; you'll instead be able to get a sense how the language works.

## ME, YOU AND EVERYBODY ELSE

The most important words in any language—in terms of how we think as much as in terms of how we construct sentences—are the personal pronouns, and especially "I" and "you". In Indonesian these words manage to be both simpler and more complicated than their English equivalents at the same time.

The best news is that the pronouns are fixed: I/me/my/ mine are all expressed with the same word. Better yet, there's no gender, so you get a single word for he/him/his/ she/her/hers. The bad news is that the social situation you're in affects which pronouns you should use.

## FORMAL

| I/me/my/mine | saya |
|---|---|
| You/your/yours | anda |

## FAMILIAR

| I/me/my/mine | aku |
|---|---|
| You/your/yours | kamu |

In this book we use both the formal and the familiar forms. Some situations—whispering sweet nothings to a boyfriend or girlfriend, for example—would only ever involve the familiar pronouns, while at other times— asking a stranger for directions, for instance—it would be highly inappropriate to use anything but the formal versions. We'll let you know at the start of each chapter whether it features "**Aku & Kamu**" (familiar) or "**Saya & Anda**" (formal) pronouns.

In practice you need to be very careful about which versions to use. Indonesians place a lot of value on respect, and blustering in too early with familiar pronouns won't create a good impression.

To make things particularly tricky, the formal/familiar versions are not perfectly matched pairs. **Anda** is particularly formal. It sounds clunky in everyday speech, and isn't used all that often. That doesn't mean you can jump straight to **kamu**, though. What Indonesians tend to do instead is use a name or a term of address as a pronoun. If you're a foreigner, a shopkeeper might ask *Mister* **mau beli apa?** ("What does mister [you] want to buy?"), and an acquaintance might ask *John* **mau makan apa?** ("What does John [you] want to eat?"). The best bet is to use this trick yourself until you hear the person you're talking to address you as **kamu**. You can then follow suit.

**Aku** is the final stage of informality, coming into play well beyond the point at which **kamu** kicks in, so in practice stick to **saya** until you hear the people you're talking to start to use **aku**.

| **He/him/his/she/her/hers** | dia |

| **You** (plural) | kalian |

Indonesian differentiates between a single and plural "you", so use **kalian** when you're addressing more than one person.

| **They/them/their/theirs** | meréka |

| **We/us/our/ours** | kami/kita |

The two versions of "we" have different uses. **Kami** is an exclusive form, used when the "we" in question *doesn't* include the person you're addressing. You might say **Kami**

**mau beli tikét** ("We want to buy a ticket") to a ticket seller at a bus terminal. **Kita** is an inclusive "we", taking in both the person speaking and the person/people spoken to, e.g., **Kita ke mana?** ("Where shall we go?") In practice, **kita** is often used to cover both bases, and the decline of the correct use of **kami** is a favorite bugbear of Indonesian grammarians.

## NYA

Related to the pronouns is the ubiquitous Indonesian suffix **nya**. This basically serves as a three-letter stand-in for any item, person, topic or issue, the identity of which is so inherently obvious in a particular conversation that it doesn't need spelling out in full. In practice this usually makes it into an indicator of possession, like "apostrophe + s" in English, with the important difference being that by using **nya**, you automatically remove the pronoun itself from the sentence. If we're talking about John, someone might say **Rumah*nya* besar banget** ("John's/his house is very big"), with the **nya** here standing in for John/**dia**. If you're not quite sure who or what the **nya** is representing, you can always ask **Rumah siapa?** ("Whose house?")—to which the reply would be, **Rumah dia! Rumah John!** ("His house! John's house!").

## DIALECT VERSIONS OF YOU AND I: LU AND GUÉ

In the dialect form of Indonesian spoken in Jakarta, **aku** is usually replaced with **gué** (or sometimes **gua**), and **kamu** turns into **lu**. These pronouns are actually borrowed from the Chinese Hokkien dialect—some indication of how much impact Chinese immigration has had on Indonesia over the centuries. It's very unusual to hear **gué/lu** used outside the capital, however, so we don't suggest you use them—you'll sound pretty ridiculous to people in Bali or Surabaya if you do!

## YES AND NO

**yes**                            ya

This tends to get stretched out, particularly if it's an emphatic yes, to become **iya**.

**no**                            tidak

**not**                            bukan

It's important to remember the difference between these two negatives. **Tidak** means "no", and is also used to negate a verb: **Aku *tidak* suka pisang** ("I don't like bananas"). **Bukan** goes only with nouns: **Itu *bukan* pisang!** ("That's not a banana!").

In colloquial Indonesian, **tidak** almost always morphs into **nggak** (don't forget to pronounce that second **g**, and to retain that unaspirated terminal **k**!). This is often further abbreviated to a simple **gak** (or occasionally **tak**), and where it comes before a word beginning with a vowel, it sometimes contracts to little more than a single consonant, **g**. In speech, the phrase **tidak apa-apa** ("no problem") usually comes out more like "**gapapa**".

## QUESTION WORDS

| | |
|---|---|
| **why** | **kenapa** |

In formal Indonesian "why" is **mengapa**, but this is rarely used in everyday speech.

| | |
|---|---|
| **what** | **apa** |
| **who** | **siapa** |
| **where** | **mana** |
| **when** | **kapan** |
| **how** | **bagaimana** |

## REPLIES AND RESPONSES

In Indonesian it's actually very unusual to reply to a question with the words **ya** ("yes") or **nggak** ("no"). It's more usual to respond using the question's main verb. So, if someone asks **Bisa bicara Bahasa Indonesia?** ("Can you speak Indonesian?"), the response is **Bisa** ("Can"), not **Ya**. Even if the response is negative, the verb should be used, so **Nggak bisa**, rather than simply **Nggak**.

Similarly, if someone asks you **Sudah makan?** ("Have you already eaten"), you would respond with **Sudah** ("Already"), or **Belum** ("Not yet"), rather than with a yes or a no.

**CANNOT!**

The Indonesian convention of using verbs to reply to questions, instead of simply responding with yes or no, has had a subtle impact on the way English is spoken in the regions of Southeast Asia where Malay (the earlier version of the language) has historically been an important language. Indonesian shopkeepers with very decent English will nonetheless often say "have" or "don't have" when you enquire about a particular item, and even in Singapore where more people speak English than Malay, "can" and "cannot" is a pretty common response!

## WORD ORDER

The order of nouns and adjectives in Indonesian is the reverse of English. "The big house" would be **rumah besar** (literally "house big"). But otherwise, the most basic kind of sentence structure is similar to English: subject-verb-object, for example **Aku makan pisang** (literally "I eat the banana"). In colloquial Indonesian, however, things get a bit looser, and word order can be chopped and changed to create emphasis and expressiveness.

| **I'm tired.** | **Aku capék.** |

This is the normal way to structure this sentence, but you might well hear someone say **Capék aku!** It's more forceful this way, and means something like "I'm totally worn out—leave me alone!"

**I can't speak English.**
(literally "I can't
English"—the verb is
often dropped in
sentences about ability
to do something).

**Aku nggak bisa
Bahasa Inggris.**

Someone might change the word order and say **Bahasa Inggris nggak bisa aku!** This is more forceful, with a note of exasperation. It might well infer something like "I have no idea what you're saying! Stop speaking English at me!"

## GETTING TENSE

"Indonesian has no tenses", you'll sometimes be told. It's certainly true that verbs don't mutate to create new forms the way they do in English, and it's also true that Indonesian relies on inference more than English. After all, even in English you don't really need to change the verb into the future tense when you say **Aku berangkat bésok** (literally "I leave tomorrow"). But there *are* tenses of a sort in Indonesian, formed by marker words, and they're sometimes essential to make your meaning clear.

**will**                                    **akan**
e.g., **Aku akan beli pisang bésok** ("I will buy bananas tomorrow")

**already**                              **sudah**
e.g., **Aku sudah makan** ("I already ate")

**not yet**                    belum

e.g., **Aku belum makan** ("I haven't eaten yet")

**ever**                       pernah

**Pernah** is an important marker for creating what would be a "present perfect tense" in English; e.g., "I have seen that film" would be **Aku pernah nonton film itu** (literally "I ever watch that film"—you'll sometimes hear Indonesian speakers saying this sort of thing in English). "Never" is simply **tidak pernah**.

**in the middle**              sedang

This word is most commonly used to mean "medium" (on a restaurant menu it would indicate a dish that's neither very spicy nor very mild). But it's also used as a tense marker to create what would be a "continuous tense" in English; e.g., **Aku *sedang* makan pisang** ("I'm in the middle of eating a banana, right at this minute!")

# YANG

When it comes to building your own Indonesian sentences, one of the most useful words is the conjunction **yang**. The closest direct translation of **yang** is something like "that which is", but it also serves to mean "the … one", "a", and more besides.

**The big one**                Yang besar

**Are there any big ones?**    Ada yang besar?

**I'm looking for a big one.**

Aku cari yang besar.

**This one or that one?**

Yang ini atau yang itu?

**Tell the truth!**
(lit., "That which is true only!")

Yang benar aja!

## BITS AND PIECES: PARTICLES

Colloquial Indonesian strips out a lot of superfluous words, which is great! Unfortunately, it has a tendency to then fill all the space with new expressive particles, a sort of linguistic shrapnel to give the syntax an extra zip and zing. The exact meanings of the different particles are often very subtle, and it's hard to consciously learn how to use them appropriately. It's really just a case of spending a long time talking to Indonesians, in Indonesian, until one day you simply find them coming out of your mouth as if it was the most natural thing in the world! We will, though, encounter some of the most common examples—**loh**, **kok**, **sih**, and **dong**—in the chapters to come, and will explain what they mean when we do.

# 2

# What's Up?

## Greetings and Sharing News with Friends

**AKU & KAMU** (familiar pronouns throughout)

| | |
|---|---|
| **Hi!** | Hai! |
| **Hello!** | Hallo! |

**Hallo** is usually more frequently used when answering the phone or trying to get someone's attention upon entering a house, office or shop and finding that no one's around.

| | |
|---|---|
| **Haven't seen you for ages!** | Lama nggak ketemu! |
| **We meet again!** | Ketemu lagi! |
| **How's things?** | Apa kabar? |

**Apa kabar** literally means "What's the news?" but it isn't really a request for information about recent happenings, and the standard response is cursory, usually along the lines of "fine", "so-so" or "not so good". If you really did want to get the news you might ask **Ada kabar?** ("Is there news?") or **Apa gosipnya?** ("What's the gossip?")

| | |
|---|---|
| **Fine** | **Baik-baik aja** |
| **So-so** | **Biasa aja** |
| **Not so good** | **Kurang baik** |

### SLANG ALERT:
## Aja/saja="just"/"only"

The word **saja** means "just". It's one of the commonly used Indonesian words that usually loses its initial consonant in informal speech, thus becoming **aja**. It can be used to mean "exactly", "completely" or "only". **Baik-baik aja** is equivalent to saying "Things are just fine!"

| | |
|---|---|
| **I've been really busy at work.** | **Aku lagi sibuk banget di kantor.** |

**Kantor** means "office"; anyone who works in an office environment will usually talk about "the office" rather than "work" (**kerja**).

| | |
|---|---|
| **I've been busy at university.** | **Aku lagi sibuk di kampus.** |

"University" is **universitas**, and "studying" is **kuliah**, but Indonesian students tend to talk about university as a physical location, namely **kampus** ("campus").

## SLANG ALERT:
# Banget/sekali/sangat="very"

**Banget** is a slang term for "very", which replaces the more formal word **sekali** after the adjective, so "very busy" is **sibuk banget**. There's another formal word for "very", **sangat**, but that one has to come before the adjective: **sangat sibuk**.

| | |
|---|---|
| **How's John?** | **Bagaimana John?** |
| **How's he/she?** | **Gimana dia?** |

In everyday speech, **Bagaimana** ("how") is usually abbreviated to **gimana**.

| | |
|---|---|
| **Any news from John?** | **Ada kabar dari John?** |
| **He's fine.** | **Dia baik.** |
| **He's sick, I think.** | **Dia lagi sakit, kayaknya.** |
| **He's on holiday!** | **Libur dia!** |

Swapping the usual word order here (**dia libur**) gives a statement like this more force.

| | |
|---|---|
| **What are you up to?** | Lagi ngapain? |
| **What are you doing here?** | Ngapain disini? |
| **Just hanging out.** | Nongkrong aja. |
| **Just taking a stroll.** | Jalan-jalan aja. |

## SLANG ALERT:
# Ngapain="What are you doing?"

**Ngapain** is a slang term, condensing a whole question—"What are you doing?"/"What are you up to?"—into a single word. It's also sometimes used to mean "Why?" especially when there's a tone of surprise or bafflement in the question; e.g., **Ngapain begitu?** ("Why are you doing it like that?!?").

## SLANG ALERT: Kayak/seperti="like"
**Kayak** is a word that's snuck out of full-blown Bahasa Gaul into everyday speech. It means "like", as in "it's like that", and it often replaces the more formal word, **seperti**. With the **nya** suffix added, **Kayaknya** means "It seems like", although it usually goes at the end of a sentence: **dia marah, kayaknya** (literally "He's angry, it seems like", but best translated as "He's angry, I think…")

| | |
|---|---|
| **What's up?** <br> (What's wrong?) | Ada apa? |

| | |
|---|---|
| **Nothing's up!** | Nggak ada apa-apa! |
| **Really?** | Oh ya? |
| **Are you serious?** | Sungguh? |
| **Seriously?!?** | Masa?!? |

Depending on your tone, **masa** can be either an expression of shock—"You're kidding!"—or an expression of scoffing disbelief—"You're talking nonsense!" The vowels tend to get slightly rounded, to become something like a cross between **a** and **o**.

| | |
|---|---|
| **Hey! I forgot to tell you!** | Eh! Aku lupa kasihtau! |
| **I forgot.** | Aku lupa/Aku lali. |

**Lupa** is the commonest word for "forget"; **lali** is more slangy (and also a bit cutesy).

| | |
|---|---|
| **Seriously, tell me the truth!** | Sériusnya, yang benar aja! |
| **Not likely!** (expressing disbelief) | Nggak mungkin!/ Mana mungkin! |

**Mungkin** means maybe, so these phrases literally mean "Not maybe!" **Nggak mungkin** is the commonest form; **mana mungkin** usually carries a slightly more forceful tone. If you flip the word order around, **mungkin nggak** simply means "maybe not".

| | |
|---|---|
| **For sure!** (Definitely!) | Memang! |

## SLANG ALERT: **Memang/pasti**

**Memang** is a slang term, meaning "certainly", or "for sure". In formal Indonesian the word **pasti** would be used instead. **Memang** itself is sometimes abbreviated to **emang**.

| | |
|---|---|
| **Okay!** | Oke! |

| | |
|---|---|
| **That's it!/That's why!** | Nah itu dia! |

This is usually used when someone has just grasped a point you've been trying to make, something equivalent to, "Now you get it!"

| | |
|---|---|
| **Oh, I see.** | Oh, gitu. |

This literally means "Oh, (it's) like that". **Gitu** is an abbreviation of **begitu**.

| | |
|---|---|
| **Cool!** | Hebat! |

| | |
|---|---|
| **Great!** (Sweet!) | Sip! |

| | |
|---|---|
| **Don't worry about it.** | Nggak apa-apa kok. |

### KOK GITU SIH!

**Kok** is one of Indonesian's many expressive particles. Put it at the front of a word and it creates a tone of questioning surprise. **Kok bisa Bahasa Indonesia?** means something like "No way! You speak Indonesian! How did you learn?"

**Kok gitu?** might mean "Woah! Why's it like that?", "She did *what?*", "Oh no! *Really?*" and lots of other things besides. Stick another expressive particle, **sih**, on the end, and the phrase will have a tone of frustration: **Kok gitu sih!** might mean something like "Why are you being like that?" or "Does it *really* have to be that way?"

Take the **kok** particle and stick it on the other end of a sentence, however, and its meaning changes, emphasizing an argument, and possibly dismissing someone's complaint or expression of concern. Someone might say, **Kok gitu?** and you might respond, **Ya gitu aja kok,** meaning something like "That's just the way it is! Get used to it!" and in the case of **kok** and its two meanings, that *is* just the way it is! Get used to it!

| | |
|---|---|
| **OK, I'm going off now.** | Oke, aku pergi dulu, ya. |
| **Do you want to come** (with us/me)? | Mau ikut? |
| **Just join** (us/me)**!** | Ikut aja dong! |

**Ikut** means "follow". It can be used to mean "follow" literally, but it can also mean "join" or "take part", as well as "follow" in a more abstract sense, as in "following" a particular sport.

| | |
|---|---|
| **See you again.** | Sampai ketemu lagi. |

This literally means "Until meeting again" or "Until we meet again"

| | |
|---|---|
| **I'll catch up with you again later.** | Ketemu lagi nanti, ya. |
| **See you soon.** | Sampai jumpa lagi. |

# 3

# Pleased to Meet You!

## Getting to Know People

**SAYA & ANDA** (formal pronouns throughout)

| | |
|---|---|
| **Good morning.** | Selamat pagi. |
| **Good day.** | Selamat siang. |
| **Good afternoon.** | Selamat soré. |
| **Good evening.** | Selamat malam. |

It takes a while to get your head around these time-specific greetings. Unlike in English, "morning" (**pagi**) ends well before midday, and there's a baggy, imprecise period around lunchtime known as **siang**, which literally means "day" (**siang-hari** means "daytime" and **malam-hari** is "night time"). Exactly when **pagi** ends and **siang** begins depends on who you are, where you are, and what job you're doing, but as a rough rule of thumb you should use **pagi** up to around 11am, and **siang** from then onwards. The point at which **siang** becomes **soré** is similarly imprecise, but by 3pm you are certainly safely into **soré** territory. At the end of the day, meanwhile, **soré** (afternoon) lingers a little longer than it would in English. You wouldn't start saying **selamat malam** until the sun has set and night has properly fallen.

**Selamat malam** literally means "good night", of course, but it doesn't convey the English meaning of that phrase. The all-purpose Indonesian phrases for goodbye (**selamat jalan/ selamat tinggal**; more details on pg 53) are used both day and night, although you can also say **selamat tidur** if someone is going directly to bed (**tidur** means "sleep").

| **Excuse me.** | Permisi. |
|---|---|

**Permisi** is a near-exact equivalent of "excuse me" in English: you can use it to politely ask someone to step aside if they're blocking your way, catch someone's attention or to preface a question to a stranger.

| **please** (requesting) | tolong |
|---|---|

**Tolong** actually means "help", but in polite Indonesian it is used as "please" would be used in English; e.g., **Tolong minta es téh lagi?** ("Please may I have another iced tea?").

| **please** (inviting) | silahkan |
|---|---|

**Silahkan** is used when inviting someone to do something, e.g., **Silahkan duduk** ("Please sit down"). It's also used when responding to a polite request. You might ask some-one, **Boléh saya duduk?** ("May I sit down?"), and they'll respond **Silahkan!** ("Please do!")

| | |
|---|---|
| **Please come in.** | Silahkan masuk. |
| **Welcome!** | Selamat datang! |
| **Thank you.** | Terima kasih. |

**Terima kasih** literally means "received-given". Colloquially it's usually abbreviated to **makasih**.

| | |
|---|---|
| **You're welcome.** | Sama-sama. |
| **sorry** | maaf |

Each letter **a** in **maaf** needs to be pronounced, creating a two-syllable word: **ma-af**. In the longer words created from the **maaf** root, such as **maafkan** (forgive), they tend to be run into a single vowel.

| | |
|---|---|
| **I'm sorry.** | Saya minta maaf. |
| **Forgive me!** | Maafkan saya! |

## TERMS OF ADDRESS

Indonesia is a country that values politeness, and that politeness underpins the way people address each other. The commonest forms of address are **Pak** (from **bapak**, literally "father" but more generally, equivalent to "sir") and **Bu** (from **ibu**, literally "mother" but equivalent to "madam").

They are appropriate for use towards anyone noticeably older than yourself, or anyone in a position of authority or a position deserving respect. You'll probably be called **Pak/Bu** by waiters or shopkeepers, even if they are older than you, and you should definitely call a policeman **Pak** even if he's younger than you!

When addressing other adults who are roughly the same age as you or younger, and who don't require over-the-top deference, there are various possible terms of address. The most useful are **Mas** (for a man) and **Mbak** (for a woman—this is a slightly tricky word to pronounce; there's no preceding vowel so you need to make the **m** sound without opening your mouth before running it straight into the **b**, something like "mmm-back"). These terms actually come from Javanese (spoken in Central and East Java and amongst transmigrant populations all over the country). There are equivalent words in other regions (**Bang** and **Neng** in Jakarta and West Java; **Bli** and **Mbok** in Bali, etc.), but **Mas** and **Mbak** are universally understood, and acceptable everywhere. They're particularly appropriate terms for addressing staff in hotels and restaurants. When talking to children, the most useful term is **Adik** (also borrowing from Javanese), which literally means "little brother/sister".

As a foreigner, you may find yourself addressed as **Om**, "uncle", or **Tanté**, "aunty", which are familiar but respectful. Occasionally you might hear the term **Tuan**, which means "master" and has uncomfortable colonial-era undertones. Most likely, though, you'll simply be called "Mister"—an English loanword which has become a sort of standard mode of address for a foreigner, whether male or female!

All of these terms of address, as well as personal names, are frequently used as stand-ins for personal pronouns, which is a good way to avoid using the clunky, hyper-formal **anda** ("you").

| | |
|---|---|
| **What's your name?** | Siapa nama anda?/ Namanya siapa? |

"Who" (**siapa**) rather than "what" (**apa**) is used when asking someone's name.

| | |
|---|---|
| **My name is [John].** | Nama saya [John]. |
| **What's his/her name?** | Siapa nama dia? |
| **His name's [John].** | Nama dia [John]/ Namanya [John]. |
| **Where are you from?** | Dari mana? |

The pronoun is often dropped in questions like this, but if you want to make it absolutely clear who you're addressing you can add **anda** (**Anda dari mana?**), **dia, kalian, meréka**, or a term of address (e.g., **Pak dari mana?**).

| | |
|---|---|
| **Where do you come from?** | Asal dari mana? |
| **Where are you originally from?** | Asli mana? |

The three questions above are all used to ask the same thing: "where are you from?" The latter two are less ambiguous than the first, making it clear that the questioner wants to know your place/country of origin.

| | |
|---|---|
| **Where do you live?** | **Tinggal dimana?** |

**NO, I MEAN WHERE ARE YOU FROM NOW!**
**Dari mana?** can be an ambiguous question. Sometimes it means "Which country are you from?" and sometimes it means "Where have you just come from?" Likewise, **Tinggal dimana?** can mean "Where's your home?" or "Where are you staying here in Indonesia?" You can always add the word **sekarang** ("now") to the question for more clarity: **Dari mana sekarang?**

| | |
|---|---|
| **I'm from…** | **Saya dari…** |
| **Britain** | **Inggris** |
| **Australia** | **Australia** |

(Remember that Indonesian pronunciation rules apply, so the first vowel sound is something that in c**ow**; the second **a** is short as in h**a**t; and the **r** is rolled.)

| | |
|---|---|
| **Canada** | **Kanada** |
| **China** | **Cina** |
| **France** | **Perancis** |
| **Germany** | **Jerman** |
| **Japan** | **Jepang** |

| | |
|---|---|
| **Netherlands** | Belanda |
| **New Zealand** | Selandia Baru |
| **Saudi Arabia** | Arab Saudi |
| **Singapore** | Singapura |
| **Spain** | Spanyol |
| **USA** | Amérika Serikat |

The names of most other countries are similar in Indonesian and English.

## HELLO BULÉ!

If you're a Caucasian foreigner in Indonesia you'll have to get used to being described as **bulé**. The word originally meant "albino", but it has become a general slang term for white people. Some foreigners living in or regularly visiting Indonesia dislike the term, but it's generally purely descriptive, and has no racist intent, even though it is an overtly racial designation.

| **What's your job?** | Kerja apa? |
|---|---|

Again, the personal pronoun will usually be dropped in this question, unless it's absolutely necessary for clarity, as in **Anda kerja apa?** ("What's *your* job?"). As a foreigner, you'll often be asked **Bisnis apa?** ("What's your business?"), the assumption being that you must be some kind of businessperson if you have enough cash to swan around the world on exotic holidays!

| | |
|---|---|
| **I'm an English teacher.** | Saya guru Bahasa Inggris. |
| **Builder** | Pembangun |
| **Bus driver** | Supir bis |
| **Businessperson** | Pengusaha |

People will also often say **Saya bisnis** ("I'm in business").

| | |
|---|---|
| **Chef** | Koki |
| **Doctor** | Dokter |
| **Government employee** | Pegawai Negeri |
| **Journalist** | Wartawan/Jurnalis |
| **Police officer** | Polisi |
| **Soldier** | Tentara |
| **Student** | Mahasiswa |

People also often say **Saya masih kuliah**, which means "I'm still studying".

| | |
|---|---|
| **I'm already retired.** | Saya sudah pensiun. |
| **Are you married?** | Sudah kawin? |
| **I'm married.** | Saya sudah kawin. |

| | |
|---|---|
| **I'm not married.** | Saya belum kawin. |
| **I'm already engaged.** | Saya sudah bertunangan. |
| **I already have a fiancé/fiancée.** | Saya sudah punya tunangan. |

When talking about fiancés/fiancées, as well as the word **tunangan** people also use the terms **calon istri** (literally "candidate wife") and **calon suami** ("candidate husband").

When asking and answering questions about marriage and family, "already" (**sudah/udah**) and "not yet" (**belum**) are the operative words. Even if you're a confirmed bachelor of 80, you are still **Belum kawin** ("Not yet married") rather than "not married".

| | |
|---|---|
| **Do you have children?** | Sudah punya anak? |

The reply to this question would always be **sudah/udah** ("already") or **belum** ("not yet") rather than yes/no.

| | |
|---|---|
| **How many children [do you have]?** | Anaknya berapa? |
| **I have [two] children.** | Saya punya [dua] anak. |
| **[One] girl and [one] boy** | [Satu] céwék, [satu] cowok |
| **girl** | céwék |
| **boy** | cowok |

**I don't have children**
**[yet]; how about you?**

Saya belum punya anak.
Gimana kalau anda?
Sudah atau belum?

## SLANG ALERT:
## Kawin/menikah="married"

**Kawin** is not strictly a slang term, but it is much less formal than the alternative word for "married", **menikah**. It actually literally means "mated", but it's perfectly polite when talking about marriage between human beings. When people use **kawin** to talk about animals, however, the inference is somewhat more blunt!

## SLANG ALERT:
## Céwék/perempuan, cowok/laki-laki= "male" and "female"

The terms **céwék** ("female") and **cowok** ("male") are slang equivalents to the more formal **perempuan** and **laki-laki**. They are not age-specific, and you'd need to say **anak perempuan/anak céwék** to make it clear you were talking about a "girl child". In the past **céwék** could occasionally carry a slightly disrespectful tone, perhaps roughly equivalent to "chick" in American slang. These days, though, it seems to have slipped across into general usage, and is appropriate for most situations. There is also another pair of words—**pria** ("man") and **wanita** ("woman"), but they're not commonly used in conversation. The only place you're likely to encounter them is on a toilet door!

| | |
|---|---|
| **How old are you?** | Umurnya berapa? |
| | Berapa usia anda? |

Both **umur** and **usia** mean "age". The question here is literally "How much is your age?"

| | |
|---|---|
| **I'm [30] years old.** | Saya [tigapuluh] tahun. |
| **I'm already really old!** | Saya sudah tua banget! |
| **Still young!** | Masih muda! |

## OLD AND NEW, YOUNG AND OLD

When talking about age, **tua** means "old", or "aged", while **muda** means "young". When talking about things, buildings, places and so on, **baru** means "new". Both **tua** ("aged") and **lama** ("long time") can be used, for example, a city's "Old Church" could be either **Geréja Lama** or **Geréja Tua**.

| | |
|---|---|
| **Are you on holiday here?** | Libur disini? |
| **For how long are you staying in Indonesia?** | Berapa lama di Indonesia? |
| **How long have you been in Indonesia already?** | Udah berapa lama di Indonesia? |
| **Are you having a good time in Indonesia?** | Énak di Indonesia, nggak? |

| | |
|---|---|
| **For sure, I'm enjoying it here!** | Memang, saya énak disini! |

## "MY BODY IS NOT DELICIOUS!"

Énak is a fun word. It's often translated as "delicious", and it certainly can be applied to food. But it also means "pleasing" in a general sense: a country can be énak to visit, and a place can be énak to work at. Nggak énak ("not pleasing") in particular can be used to express feeling uncomfortable or ill at ease in a place or situation, e.g., **Saya nggak énak disana** ("I wasn't comfortable there"). Énak is also used to talk about physical sensations, and if someone has a fever they might well say **Badan saya nggak énak**— which Indonesians frequently, and hilariously, translate into English as "My body is not delicious!"

## ASKING THE UNASKABLE

In Indonesia there are certain questions that you may well be asked within a few minutes of meeting someone for the first time, which no one would ever dare to ask back home. These typically include: **Umurnya berapa?** ("How old are you?"), followed rapidly by **Udah kawin?** ("Are you already married?") and **Kenapa?** ("Why not?") if the answer's "no"; **Gajinya berapa?** ("How much do you earn?") asked as an automatic follow-up to "What's your job?"; and **Agamanya apa?** ("What's your religion?") if you're uncomfortable answering any of these questions, the best bet is simply to laugh and make a joke of it. You could reply **Tua banget!** ("Really old!") or **Masih muda!** ("Still young!") to the age enquiry, or **Nggak cukup!** ("Not enough!") to the query about your salary.

Do remember, though, that there's absolutely nothing impertinent about these questions in an Indonesian cultural context, and Indonesians will almost always be unfussed about answering them themselves.

## WHAT'S YOUR RELIGION?

**Agamanya apa?** ("What's your religion?") is a standard Indonesian question. For Indonesians, the answer will be that they are a follower of one of the country's six officially sanctioned faiths: **Islam**; **Kristen** (specifically Protestant Christian); **Katolik** (Catholic); **Hindu**; **Buda** (Buddhist); or **Konghucu** (Confucian). These terms are used for both the religion itself, its followers, and as an adjective, so **Saya Konghucu** means "I'm a Confucian"; **Itu klenteng Konghucu** means "That's a Confucian temple"; and **Agama Konghucu** means "Confucianism" (Muslim Indonesians may say either **Saya Islam** or **Saya Muslim**, both meaning "I'm a Muslim").

It's not that other religions are *illegal*; it's just that they're not an option for official acknowledgement. Words for other international religions include **Yahudi** (Jew/Jewish/ Judaism) and **Sik** (Sikh/Sikhism). Although there's a certain amount of political hostility towards Israel in Indonesia, it's nowhere near as much of a popular preoccupation as it is in the Middle East, and the vast majority of Indonesians will be intrigued, rather than hostile, if you tell them you're Jewish. However, if you say that you're **atéis** (atheist) or **agnostis** (agnostic) you're likely to be met with bafflement and sometimes even hostility. There *are* a handful of self-declared Indonesian atheists, but mainstream Indonesian society tends to view them, rightly or wrongly, as willfully provocative rebels. This attitude is by no means entirely down to strictly religious sentiment: in diverse Indonesia someone's religious designation tends to be a key part of their identity, and even people who never practice their religion—and who may not even really believe in its tenets—will usually still automatically call themselves **Kristen**, **Muslim** or whatever it may be. Naturally, then, if you come from a broadly Catholic heritage, for example, they'd expect you to say **Saya Katolik**, "I'm a Catholic"—in much the same way, in fact, as many non-religious Jews still call themselves "Jewish"…

## FOTO MISTER!

**"Foto mister! Foto sama aku!"** If you're a foreigner visiting a major domestic tourist destination, chances are you'll hear this request from every gaggle of excitable young sightseers you encounter: "Photo, mister! Take a photo with me!" Indonesians love selfies (in fact, the word "selfie" has entered the Indonesian language) and group photos, and a six-foot Westerner or a stylishly dressed Northeast Asian certainly makes an eye-catching addition to the holiday album. It's entirely good-natured, though when you're up to the fifth photo request in as many minutes it can get a bit tiring. The only thing you can do is respond with a smile—particularly if people have taken the time to ask you politely: **Permisi mister, boléh kami ambil foto sama mister?** ("Excuse me, mister; may we take a photo with mister?"

**Goodbye**                     Selamat jalan
   (to a person leaving)

**Goodbye**                     Selamat tinggal
   (to a person remaining)

Colloquially people also often say **da-da**, or simply **da**, as a way of saying goodbye.

**It's been nice meeting**      Senang bertemu dengan
   **you.**                        anda.

# 4

# Hey There!

## Understandings, Misunderstandings and Disagreements

**AKU & KAMU** (familiar pronouns throughout)

Is there a problem?     Ada masalah?

What's wrong with you? Ada apa sama kamu?

There's nothing wrong   Nggak ada apa-apa
    with me!              sama aku tau!

### SLANG ALERT: **Sama/dengan="with"**

**Sama** is not a slang word in itself. It means "same" or "both". In verb form, **bersama**, it means "to be together". **Berangkat bersama dengan aku** means "Let's leave together" (lit., "Leave together with me"). However, in colloquial Indonesian this almost always contracts to

**Berangkat sama aku.** What's more, colloquially **sama** also tends to replace **dengan** "with" in sentences such as **Ada apa dengan kamu?**

### SLANG ALERT: **Tau!!! = "You know!!!"**

**Tau** is an abbreviation of **tahu** ("know"). Using it at the end of a sentence creates a tone of somewhat bad-tempered forcefulness: **Aku capék tau!** or "I'm tired, you know!" Even more forceful is the phrase **Tau nggak sih!** It literally means "Do you know or not?" but it carries a lot more force than that. **Aku capék, tau nggak sih!** probably translates best into something along the lines of "Get it through your thick skull—I'm tired!"

| | |
|---|---|
| **What are you talking about?** | Kamu omong apa? |
| **What did you say?** | Kamu bilang apa? |
| **I didn't say anything!** | Aku nggak bilang apa-apa! |
| **Did you hear me or not?** | Denger apa nggak? |
| **I didn't hear.** | Aku nggak denger. |

The correct spelling and pronunciation of the word for "hear" is **dengar**, but this is an instance where a final **a** often becomes an **e** in colloquial Indonesian.

**SLANG ALERT:**
## Omong/bicara, bilang/kata="speak", "say"

**Omong** is the slang equivalent of **bicara** "speak", with **ngomong** being the full verb counterpart to **berbicara**. Meanwhile, **bilang** is the slang for "say". In formal Indonesian "to say" is **berkata**. The root here, **kata**, literally means "word", but it's also used interchangeably with **bilang** as a colloquial way of saying "say," thus "I said" would be **Aku kata/Aku bilang**.

### SLANG ALERT: Apa/atau="or"

**Atau** means "or" as in **kamu atau aku**, "you or me". In very colloquial Indonesian, however, **apa**, which usually means "what" gets used in its place, as in **Denger apa nggak?** ("Did you hear or not?")

**I don't understand.**   **Aku nggak ngerti.**

Verb forms beginning with **meng** tend to lose their first two letters in colloquial Indonesian. **Mengerti** ("to understand") often becomes **ngerti**.

**What do you mean?**   **Apa maksudmu?**

The familiar pronouns **aku** and **kamu** can be abbreviated and tagged onto the preceding word. **Maksud** is "meaning", so **maksudku** is "my meaning" (often used to say "I mean") and **maksudmu** is "your meaning".

| | |
|---|---|
| **What do you mean?** | Maksudmu apa? |
| **What I mean is this:** [explanation follows] | Maksudku begini... |
| **That's what he/she said.** | Gitu katanya. |
| **It has to be like that.** | Harus begitu. |
| **It should be like this.** | Mestinya begini. |
| **Don't be like that!** | Jangan begitu! |

**Jangan** is the word used for creating all negative impera-tives, e.g., **Jangan duduk!** ("Don't sit down!"). Positive imperatives in formal Indonesian can be created with the suffix **lah**, e.g., **Duduklah!** ("Sit down!"). In the colloquial language, however, **saja/aja** ("just") is often used instead: **Duduk aja!** ("Just sit down!")

| | |
|---|---|
| **Just shut up!** | Diam aja! |
| **I can't understand your Indonesian, speak English!** | Aku nggak ngerti Bahasa Indonesiamu, omong Bahasa Inggris aja! |
| **I can only speak a little English!** | Aku cuman bisa sedikit Bahasa Inggris! |

## SLANG ALERT: **Cuma/hanya="only"**

**Cuma**—which often picks up an *n* at the end to become **cuman**—is a colloquial word for "only". Its more formal equivalent is **hanya**. Unlike **saja/aja**, **cuman/hanya** go before the thing they refer to in a sentence: **Aku cuman bisa sedikit Bahasa Inggris; Aku bisa sedikit Bahasa Inggris aja** or "I can only speak a little English".

**Cuman** can also be used to mean "it's just that…", e.g., **Aku mau beli, cuman aku nggak punya uang!** ("I'd like to buy it, it's just that I haven't got any money!")

| | |
|---|---|
| **So what should we do? What's to be done?** | Terus gimana? |
| **So what do you want to do about it?** | Mau gimana lagi? |

Both of these phrases convey a slight sense of frustration, rather like saying "It seems there's nothing to be done; so what do *you* suggest?!?"

| | |
|---|---|
| **It's up to you.** | Terserah kamu. Terserah! |

On its own, **terserah** conveys a tone of throwing up your hands and walking away, a bit like saying, "Do what you want; I couldn't care less!" (The root of the word is actually connected to the idea of "surrender".)

| | |
|---|---|
| **Whatever! Who cares!** | Biarin! |
| **I want to complain.** | Aku mau komplén. |

The verb **mengadu** also means "to complain", but when talking about "making a complaint" it's normal to use the English loanword **komplén**.

| | |
|---|---|
| **Yes, that's true.** | Iya, itu bener. |

"True" is correctly spelled and pronounced **benar**, but this is another word where the final-syllable **a** turns to **e** colloquially.

| | |
|---|---|
| **Correct!** | Betul! |
| **I know** | Aku tau |
| **Enough already!** | Ya udah! |

**Udah** (short for **sudah**, "already") is one of the most ubiquitous Indonesian words, and nothing better wraps up a pointless argument that's going nowhere than the phrase **Ya udah!**

## LOST IN TRANSLATION

English is increasingly widely spoken at a basic level in Indonesia. But outside of the urban elite, and beyond the confines of the tourist industry it's unusual to meet people who are truly fluent. The English that is spoken in Indonesia often picks up some unusual structural and vocab-related features direct from Indonesian in what's technically known as "first language interference". It's common to hear Indonesians speaking English reply with a verb, rather than yes/no, in a direct echo of their own first language—"Can you play guitar?" "Cannot!"

The fact that there are no gendered pronouns in Indonesia also causes trouble for local English speakers, and even those speaking the language at a high level occasionally suffer a lapse of concentration and confuse "he" and "she". The very different ways of creating tenses in the two languages also leads to interference. Most Indonesian English speakers have little difficulty with the simple English future tense using "will", because it closely mirrors their own version (using the marker *akan*), but when it comes to the perfect tenses, it's very common to hear Indonesians say things like "I ever go to Bali", an error caused by directly translating the Indonesian tense marker *pernah* as "ever".

Of course, language interference cuts both ways, and native English speakers learning in Indonesia make many equivalent mistakes of their own. Perhaps the most general case of first language interference from English is the tendency to massively over-construct sentences, clinging doggedly to the pronouns and superfluous verbs that would always be cast aside by a native Indonesian speaker. Strangely enough, new learners of Indonesian almost always use more words than they need to!

# 5

# Got a Minute?

## Numbers, Times, Dates and Making Plans

**SAYA & ANDA** (formal pronouns throughout)

| | |
|---|---|
| **How much/how many?** | Berapa? |
| **How many are there?** **How much is there?** | Ada berapa? |
| **number** | nomor |
| **total** | jumlah |
| **approximately** | kira-kira |
| **lots** | banyak |
| **a little** | sedikit |

## NUMBERS

| | |
|---|---|
| **0** | nol/kosong |
| **1** | satu |
| **2** | dua |
| **3** | tiga |
| **4** | empat |
| **5** | lima |
| **6** | enam |
| **7** | tujuh |
| **8** | delapan |
| **9** | sembilan |
| **10** | sepuluh |
| **11** | sebelas |
| **12** | duabelas |

Indonesian numbers follow a very logical system as they climb: **-belas** is "-teen", and from 12-19 you simply prefix **-belas** with the relevant number; 14 is **empatbelas**; 19 is **sembilanbelas**, and so on.

Equivalent to an English "-ty", as in "seven-ty", is -**puluh**. As with the 'teens', you simply prefix the -**puluh** with the relevant number: 20 is **duapuluh**; 50 is **limapuluh**. You then add the second part of the number: 22 is **duapuluh-dua**.

"Hundred" is **ratus**, so 400 is **empat ratus**. "Thousand" is **ribu**, so 6,000 is **enam ribu**, and 324,000 is **tiga-ratus-duapuluh-empat-ribu**. "Million", meanwhile, is **juta**, so 2 million is **dua juta**.

The only thing to remember is that in numbers of two digits or more, an initial "1" is usually represented by **se-** rather than **satu**: 10 is **sepuluh**; 100 is **seratus**; 1,000 is **seribu**. The only exception is "million", where 1 million is **satu juta**.

| | |
|---|---|
| **31** | tigapuluh-satu |
| **99** | sembilanpuluh-sembilan |
| **100** | seratus |
| **400** | empat ratus |
| **1,200** | seribu dua-ratus |
| **3,000** | tiga ribu |
| **1 million** | satu juta |
| **2 million** | dua juta |

## ORDINAL NUMBERS & FRACTIONS

To create ordinal numbers (first, second, third etc.) you
simply add the prefix **ke-**, e.g., "second" is **kedua**; "fiftieth" is
**kelimapuluh**. A notable exception is "first", which is
**pertama**.

| | |
|---|---|
| **half** | setengah |
| **third** | sepertiga |
| **quarter** | seperempat |
| **three-quarters** | tiga-perempat |
| **all** | semua |

## TIME

| | |
|---|---|
| **hour** | jam |
| **minute** | menit |
| **day** | hari |
| **week** | minggu |
| **month** | bulan |
| **year** | tahun |

**Jam** means both "hour" and "o' clock" in English. "Five
o'clock" is **jam lima**. To say "ten past five" you say **jam lima**

léwat sepuluh (**léwat** means "past"); to say "ten to five" you say **jam lima kurang sepuluh** (**kurang** means "less"). The only confusion comes with "half past": **setengah lima** literally translates as "half five", but it actually means 4.30.

If this is confusing you can always just stick to the 24-hour clock, where 5.10 is simply, and 5.50 is **lima-limapuluh**.

| | |
|---|---|
| **five o'clock in the morning** | jam lima pagi |
| **five o'clock in the afternoon** | jam lima sore |
| **ten o'clock at night** | jam sepuluh malam |
| **time** | waktu |

**Waktu** literally means "time", but it can also be used to mean "when" while talking about events in the past. **Waktu saya di Bali** would mean "When I was in Bali", or more literally "One time when I was in Bali…"

## DAYS & DATES

| | |
|---|---|
| **Monday** | Senin |
| **Tuesday** | Selasa |
| **Wednesday** | Rabu |
| **Thursday** | Kamis |

| Friday | Jumat |
|---|---|
| Saturday | Sabtu |
| Sunday | Hari Minggu |

You can simply say **Minggu** for "Sunday", but **minggu** is also the word for "week", so **Hari Minggu** (literally "Sunday Day") avoids confusion.

| today | hari ini |
|---|---|
| yesterday | kemarin |
| tomorrow | bésok |
| **What's the date today?** | Tanggal berapa hari ini? |
| **When** (lit., **What date) are we going to Jakarta?** | Tanggal berapa kita ke Jakarta? |

Indonesian dates are constructed British-style (day-month-year), and feature regular rather than ordinal numbers (in Indonesian you say "16 December", not "16th December). Years are said as in English, so 1999 would be **sembilanbelas-sembilanpuluh-sembilan** ("nineteen-ninety-nine"), or, in the full formal version **sembilanbelas-ratus-sembilanpuluh-sembilan** ("nineteen-hundred-and-ninety-nine"). To say a year in the 21st century, i.e., 2017, this would be **dua ribu-tujuhbelas**. The date of Indonesia's Declaration of Independence would read like this:

| 17 August 1945 | Tujuhbelas Agustus Sembilanbelas-ratus-empatpuluh-lima |
|---|---|

## THERE'S ALWAYS TOMORROW!

Indonesian notions of **bésok** "tomorrow" and **kemarin** "yesterday" can be a little imprecise. Usually when people are talking about **kemarin** they do indeed mean "the day before today"—but not always. **Kemarin** could just as easily be the middle of last week, and occasionally some time long before that. You might express shock when someone tells you there was a tiger in the village "yesterday", but they'll then roll their eyes and say, **Maksud saya kemarin dulu!** They're talking about **kemarin dulu**, "the yesterday of the past", which might well be years ago!

Likewise, **bésok** doesn't always mean "the day after today". If someone says **bésok pagi**, they usually do mean "tomorrow morning", but otherwise it's always best to pin them down. Most phrasebooks will tell you that **depan** means "next" and **rabu depan** means "next Wednesday". But even if it's Saturday today, when someone says **bésok** they could possibly really mean "next Wednesday". If you want to be sure, always check that they mean **bésok-bésok**, ("actual tomorrow") or **bésok-rabu** ("tomorrow-Wednesday")!

| | |
|---|---|
| **next** | depan |
| **next month** | bulan depan |
| **last** | lalu |

**last month**                    bulan lalu

Indonesian months are very similar to their English equivalents.

| | |
|---|---|
| **January** | Januari |
| **February** | Februari |
| **March** | Maret |
| **April** | April |
| **May** | Méi |
| **June** | Juni |
| **July** | Juli |
| **August** | Agustus |
| **September** | Séptémber |
| **October** | Oktober |
| **November** | Novémber |
| **December** | Desémber |

## TALKING TIME

| | |
|---|---|
| **What time is it [now]?** | Jam berapa [sekarang]? |
| **How many hours?** | Berapa jam? |
| **Roughly what time will we arrive?** | Kira-kira jam berapa kita datang? |

**Kira-kira** means "roughly" or "approximately"; you can also use the word **sekitar** ("around") in the same way.

| | |
|---|---|
| **How long is the journey?** | Perjalanannya berapa jam? |
| **Wait a moment.** | Tunggu sebentar. |
| **schedule** | jadwal |
| **on time** | pada waktu |
| **late** | telat |

### SLANG ALERT: Telat/terlambat="late"

Indonesians love an abbreviation, and if they can trim a few syllables off a word, you can be sure they will! **Telat** ("late") is a good example. In this case the five middle letters of the full word—**terlambat**—have simply been taken out.

## BETTER LATE THAN NEVER

We won't make a joke about it, but the fact is there's really no such thing as "early" in Indonesian! There's a word for "early in the morning"—**pagi-pagi**. There's also the word **awal**, which means "early" as in "beginning of": **awal bulan Juni** means "early in June". But if you find yourself talking about an event that will be taking place early, then the best you can do is use **sebelum waktunya**, which means "before its time".

| plan | rencana |
|------|---------|

**Rencana** is a noun in formal Indonesian, and it is also the root from which the full verb "to plan" is built: **merencanakan**. In colloquial Indonesian, however, the noun is also used as a verb:

**I'm planning to go to Jakarta tomorrow.**    Saya rencana ke Jakarta bésok.

This literally means "I plan to Jakarta tomorrow". In sentences about travel the verb **pergi** ("to go") is often dropped, with the preposition **ke** ("to") being enough to carry the idea of a journey. **Saya pernah ke Bandung** literally translates as "I ever to Bandung"; what it actually means is "I've been to Bandung".

**Can you do it today?**    Bisa hari ini nggak?
(Is it possible today?)

**How about tomorrow?**    Kalau bésok gimana?

| | |
|---|---|
| **When can you do it?** | Kapan saja bisa? |
| (When will it be possible?) | |
| **Are you ready?** | Sudah siap? |
| **Let's go!** | Ayo! |
| **another time** | lain kali |
| **always** | selalu |
| **forever** | untuk selamanya |
| **whenever** | kapan-kapan aja |
| **later** | nanti |

## NANTI AJA!

They are dreaded phrases for anyone who likes to get things done quickly: **nanti aja** and **bésok aja**. They literally mean "just later" and "just tomorrow", and they contain that word **saja/aja** in yet another of its many subtly different uses. Here **aja** conveys the idea of dismissing the matter in hand, brushing it aside. You might demand to know **Kapan diurusin?** ("When will it be organized?"). The answer might well be **nanti aja**, or worse yet **bésok aja**! And if you continue to get stressed about it, and to demand things be done right now, then you'll probably be told **Santai aja** ("Just relax")…

# 6

# On the Road

## Language for Traveling

**SAYA & ANDA** (formal pronouns throughout)

| | |
|---|---|
| **Where do you want to go?** (Where are you going?) | Mau ke mana? |

| | |
|---|---|
| **I want to go to Surabaya.** | Mau ke Surabaya. |

**Mau ke mana** literally means "want to where?" As is often the case, the preposition **ke** ("to") can stand in here for the verb **pergi** ("to go").

| | |
|---|---|
| **What's the quickest means of transport from Jakarta to Bandung?** | Jakarta ke Bandung lebih cepat naik apa? |

| | |
|---|---|
| **by bus** | naik bis |
| **by train** | naik keréta api |
| **by airplane** | naik pesawat |
| **by ship** | naik kapal |
| **by car** | naik mobil |
| **by bicycle** | naik sepéda |
| **by motorbike** | naik motor |

Motorbike is **sepéda motor**, but this is commonly abbreviated to **motor**—literally "motor".

| | |
|---|---|
| **On foot!** | Jalan kaki! |

### GETTING AROUND TOWN

Within Indonesian cities there are usually various transport options, with varying levels of comfort! These days most **taksi** (taxis) are modern and air-conditioned, and most drivers use the meter without quibbling. If you're brave and it's rush hour you could also hop on the back of an **ojék**, a motorbike taxi. These days, both taxis and **ojék**, as well as private cars, can be hailed in most Indonesian cities using the GO-JEK and GrabCar apps, which have done away with the need for haggling, reduced prices, and made getting around urban areas a hassle-free cinch. The most traditional urban transport is the **bécak** (cycle-rickshaw), still available in some cities, away from main highways. Most cities also have public minibuses—known as **bémo** or **angkot**—running along fixed routes for fixed fares.

### AYO! NAIK!

The word **naik** literally means "go up". **Naik gunung** means "go up a mountain". But it's also used when talking about means of transport. **Naik bis** means "to go by bus"; **Saya mau ke Bandung naik bis** means "I want to go to Bandung by bus". When you're actually traveling by bus, however, you'll also hear **naik** used in a different sense, this time as an imperative meaning "Get on board!" as the bus pulls out of the terminal and the last passengers scramble inside: **Ayo! Naik!** "Come on! Get on board!"

| | |
|---|---|
| **ticket** | tikét/karcis |
| **Where can I get a ticket?** | Dimana bisa dapat tikét? |
| **here** | disini |
| **there** | disana |
| **ticket counter** | lokét |
| **Where's the ticket counter?** | Lokétnya dimana? |
| **one way** | sekali jalan |

| | |
|---|---|
| **return** | **pulang-pergi** |
| | (literally "come home-go") |
| **cancel** | **batal** |
| **canceled** | **dibatalkan** |

The English loanword—written and pronounced as in English "*kansel*"—is also becoming increasingly common, sometimes made passive according to normal Indonesian grammar rules: **dicancel** ("canceled").

### DAPAT/BELI = "GET"/"BUY"

**Dapat** means "to be able to [do something]", but it can also mean "get" or "obtain", and colloquially it often replaces **beli** "buy". **Beli dimana?** means "Where did you buy that?" **Dapat dimana?** means "Where did you get that?"

| | |
|---|---|
| **Tickets are sold out!** | Tikétnya habis! |

**Habis** is a much-used word in Indonesian—and one you don't really want to hear! It means "finished" or "all gone", and it can be used for everything from bus tickets to food. Are there any seats for the show? **Habis!** Colloquially it tends to lose the first letter, so it sounds more like **abis**, with a strong stress on the first syllable: **aaa-bis!**

| | |
|---|---|
| **Are there still tickets for tomorrow?** | Masih ada tikét buat bésok? |
| **There are!** | Ada! |

**How much is the fare?**   Ongkosnya berapa?

**Harga** means price, which you can always use when talking about transport costs, but there is also a specific word for "fare"—**ongkos.**

| | |
|---|---|
| **I want to leave tomorrow.** | Mau berangkat bésok. |
| **I want to leave tomorrow morning.** | Mau berangkat bésok pagi. |
| **I want to leave today.** | Mau berangkat hari ini. |
| **I want to leave this afternoon.** | Mau berangkat nanti soré. |
| **I want to leave now!** | Mau berangkat sekarang! |
| **What time does it leave?** | Berangkat jam berapa? |
| **What time does it reach its destination?** | Sampai tujuan jam berapa? |
| **How many hours is it to Bandung?** | Berapa jam ke Bandung? |
| **How many kilometers is it to Bandung?** | Berapa kilométer ke Bandung? |
| **How far?** | Berapa jauh? |

| | |
|---|---|
| **How long?** (strictly referring to time) | Berapa lama? |
| **Can I bring my luggage?** | Barang saya bisa dibawa? |
| **Can I get my luggage?** | Barang saya bisa diambil? |
| **Where's my luggage?** | Barang saya dimana? |

## BY BUS

| | |
|---|---|
| **bus station** | terminal |

A bus station is almost always called a "terminal"; **stasiun** ("station") almost always refers to a train station. A stop on a local bus route is a **halté**.

| | |
|---|---|
| **Which bus is for Medan?** | Bis yang mana ke Médan? |
| **Is this a direct bus?** | Ini bis langsung? |
| **Via where?** | Léwat mana? |
| **I want to get down in [Blitar].** | Saya mau turun di [Blitar]. |
| **Will you let me known when we're already in Blitar?** | Kalau udah sampai Blitar kasihtau, ya? |
| **Have we already passed Blitar?** | Udah léwat Blitar belum? |

## SLANG ALERT:
# Kasihtau/beritahu="tell"

**Beritahu** literally means "give-know", which translates as "tell". In colloquial Indonesian it usually gets replaced by **kasihtau**, which means exactly the same thing.

### STOP!

The word for "to stop" in formal Indonesian is **berhenti**, and you can certainly use this when telling a bus or taxi driver to "Stop here": **Berhenti disini**. In practice, however, Indonesians are as likely to use the English loanword, "*s-top*" (in Indonesian pronunciation a faint break appears between the *s* and *t*). You might also hear people saying **kiri**, which actually means "left", but to a bus driver the word means "Pull in! [on the left]".

## BY TRAIN

| | |
|---|---|
| **train** | keréta api |
| | (literally "fire carriage") |

People tend to simply say **keréta**, which will be understood as "train".

| | |
|---|---|
| **Do I have to change trains or not?** | Harus ganti keréta apa nggak? |
| **It's direct.** | Ini langsung aja. |
| **You have to change in Surabaya.** | Harus ganti di Surabaya. |

| | |
|---|---|
| **Which platform does the Malang train leave from?** | Yang ke Malang berangkat péron mana? |
| **platform** | péron |

At train stations it's also common to hear people use the word **jalur** (literally "lane") instead of **péron** ("platform").

| | |
|---|---|
| **Where is Carriage 3?** | Keréta Tiga dimana? |
| **Where's executive class?** | Kelas eksekutif dimana? |
| **Which station is this?** | Ini stasiun apa? |
| **How long will it take [to Malang]?** | Berapa jam [ke Malang]? |

## RIDING THE RAILS

There are basically three classes of intercity train travel available in Indonesia (train travel is mainly limited to Java, with a few lines in Sumatra). **Eksekutif** or "executive class" has comfortable reclining seats in air-conditioned carriages; **bisnis** or "business class" has padded upright seats in non-AC carriages; and **ekonomi** or "economy class" has hard upright seats and no AC. Express trains usually only feature **eksekutif** and **bisnis**.

# BY PLANE

**airport**                    bandara

In full, "airport" would be **bandara udara**. In practice, it's enough to say **bandara**, which literally means "port". For the place where you find boats, people would usually use **pelabuhan** "harbor" or **bandara laut** "sea port".

| | |
|---|---|
| **airplane** | pesawat |
| **flight** | penerbangan |
| **passenger** | penumpang |
| **arrivals** | kedatangan |
| **departures** | keberangkatan |
| **check in** | cék in |

**Passengers for flight [GA123] destined for [Denpasar] are requested to board the aircraft via gate [2].**

Para penumpang penerbangan [GA123] dengan tujuan [Denpasar], dipersilakan naik ke pesawat melalui pintu [dua].

This is the sort of hyper-formal, hyper-polite Indonesian announcement you'll hear over airport PA systems—not the kind of thing a person would ever say in real-life conversations!

## ASKING DIRECTIONS

| | |
|---|---|
| **Excuse me, could I ask you something...** | Permisi, ya; minta tanya... |
| **Where's...?** | Dimana...? |
| **Is there a [hotel] near here?** | Ada [hotél] dekat sini? |
| **What street is this?** | Ini jalan apa? |
| **How do I get there?** | Gimana ke sana? |
| **What's the address?** | Apa alamatnya? |
| **Is it still a long way?** | Masih jauh? |
| **No! You're nearly there!** | Nggak! Udah dekat! |
| **turn right** | bélok kanan |
| **turn left** | bélok kiri |
| **go straight** | jalan lurus aja |
| **Take a map so you don't get lost!** | Bawa péta biar nggak sesat di jalan! |
| **mosque** | mesjid |
| **church** | geréja |

| | |
|---|---|
| **temple (Chinese)** | klénténg |
| **temple (Hindu)** | pura |
| **shop** | toko |
| **mall** | mal |
| **post office** | kantor pos |
| **petrol station** | pompa bénsin |
| **hospital** | rumah sakit |
| **intersection** | simpang jalan |
| **When you reach [the post office], turn right.** | Kalau udah sampai [kantor pos], bélok kanan. |

## SLANG ALERT: Biar/supaya="so that"

The formal Indonesian word meaning "so that" is **supaya** as in **Minum air supaya tidak haus!** ("Drink water so that you don't get thirsty!") In colloquial speech, however, it's more likely that you'll hear people using **biar** (**Minum air biar nggak haus!**)

# 7

# Eat, Drink and Be Merry

## Food Talk

**SAYA & ANDA** (formal pronouns throughout)

**Have you eaten?**    Udah makan belum?

This is the classic **udah-belum** question, literally translating as "Already eaten not yet?" The response, naturally, is either **belum** ("not yet") or **udah** ("already").

| | |
|---|---|
| **I'm really hungry!** | Saya lapar banget! |
| **Do you want to eat?** | Mau makan? |
| **What do you want to eat?** | Mau makan apa? |
| **I want to eat** | Saya péngén makan |

## SLANG ALERT: Péngén/mau="want"

The commonest word for "to want" is **mau**, though you'll also hear the slightly more formal word **ingin**, which has the same meaning. But in colloquial Indonesian people often use **péngén** instead, which is slightly more forceful—**saya péngén makan** might mean "I *really* want to eat…"

| | |
|---|---|
| **breakfast** | sarapan |
| **lunch** | makan siang |
| **dinner** | makan malam |

### MAKAN DULU...

Indonesia is a very polite country, and it's customary to ask permission before eating in the company of others who aren't eating at the same time as you. This would even apply to a person you've been chatting to at a food stall while waiting for your order to be prepared.

The normal way to go about this is to say **Makan dulu, ya?** once the food's in front of you. This literally means "I'll eat beforehand, OK?" The response might be **Silahkan** ("Please!"), an emphatic **Mari** ("You may!"), or simply **Ya, ya, ya,** said in a way that sounds strangely dismissive to the ears of English speakers, but doesn't to Indonesians.

### EATING, INDONESIAN-STYLE

Formal sit-down meals don't often happen at home in Indonesia. Cooked food is simply left out on the side, and people help themselves whenever they're hungry. If you're invited to an Indonesian home, don't be surprised if you're offered food without anyone else joining you to eat. You're not really being done any special sort of honor; it's just that the members of the household have probably already eaten, or will eat later. If Indonesians eat as a group it's almost always outside of the home—whether at a simple food stall or an upmarket restaurant. And make no mistake—this is a country that loves to eat out!

## EATING OUT

| | |
|---|---|
| **What do you want to order?** | Mau pesan apa? |
| **Is there a menu?** | Ada menu?<br>Ada daftar makanan? |
| **Do you have…?** | Ada…? |
| **I'll have the *nasi goréng* [fried rice] and an iced tea.** | Buat saya, nasi goréngnya satu, sama es téh manisnya satu. |

There are various ways of saying what you want to order from a menu. You could simply say **Saya/Kami mau** ("I/We want") and then the items you want to order. You could be more formal and say **Saya mau pesan…** ("I want to order…"). You could also say **Minta** ("I ask for") and then what you want, which is nice and polite. But an authentic way to order—and one that you'll often hear Indonesians using—is to say the item you want + **nya** + the number you want, for example: **Karé ayamnya satu, sama nasih putih-nya dua**; "One chicken curry and two plain rice".

| | |
|---|---|
| **Is this one spicy?** | **Pedas nggak ini?** |
| **Do you have something spicy?** | **Ada yang pedas?** |
| **more spicy** | **lebih pedas** |
| **less spicy** | **kurang pedas** |
| **salty** | **asin** |
| **hot** (temperature) | **hangat/panas** |

**Hangat** is usually translated as "warm", but when talking about food it doesn't necessarily mean less hot than *panas*, the usual word for "hot". For drinks in particular, it's the more appropriate word. You wouldn't, however, describe the weather as **hangat**.

| | |
|---|---|
| **chicken** | **ayam** |
| **duck** | **bébék** |
| **beef** | **daging sapi** |
| **pork** | **daging babi** |
| **fish** | **ikan** |

| | |
|---|---|
| **crab** | kepiting |
| **prawns** | udang |
| **squid** | cumi-cumi |
| **vegetables** | sayuran |
| **cheese** | kéju |
| **egg** | telur |
| **What do you recommend?** | Ada yang bisa dirékomendasikan? |

This is one of the passive constructs that are so common in Indonesian, literally "What is there that can be recommended?" You could use an active sentence here too: **Apa yang anda bisa rékomendasikan?** (lit., "What do you recommend?"). However, there's a faint hint of impoliteness in addressing people directly in this way, so the passive voice is usually preferred.

## INDONESIAN DISHES

Many travelers think that **nasi goréng** (fried rice) and **saté** (miniature kebabs, usually of chicken, but sometimes of other meats) is the sum total of Indonesian cuisine, but there's much more on the menu than that, with a wonderful array of regional specialties and nationwide favorites. Here are a few dishes to look out for:

**Nasi pecel**    a Javanese specialty, with a tangy peanut sauce served over fresh greens and steamed rice, plus crispy crackers known as **péyék**

**Gado-gado**    an array of fresh veggies with peanut sauce

**Gudeg**    a sweet curry made from jackfruit, a local specialty in Yogyakarta

**Bakso**    meatball and noodle soup, a ubiquitous street food staple

**Soto**    a hearty soup, which comes in many forms; **soto ayam** "chicken soup" is the commonest

**Opor ayam**    a mild but flavorsome chicken and coconut curry

**Babi guling**    Balinese roast pork, laden with spices

**Martabak**    this crispy snack, something like an omelet wrapped in a crêpe, is a street food favorite

**Nasi Padang**     more an entire complex cuisine than a single dish, Padang food (which originates in the Sumatran city of the same name) features a smorgasbord of meat, fish and veggie curries, served with rice; the ultimate Padang dish is rendang, a rich, slow-cooked curry of beef or buffalo.

| | |
|---|---|
| **Can you make it without [chili]?** | Bisa dimasak tanpa [cabé]? |
| **I'm allergic to [peanuts].** | Saya alergi sama [kacang]. |
| **I don't eat meat.** | Saya nggak bisa makan daging. |
| **I'm vegetarian/vegan.** | Saya véjitarian/végan. |

Good luck with this one! Vegetarianism/veganism are unusual concepts in Indonesia, and may not be understood at all, especially at street stalls. However, the idea of cultural constraints on diet are well understood in this Muslim-majority nation, so you'll probably be better off just saying "I cannot/may not eat meat": **Saya nggak bisa/boléh makan daging.**

| | |
|---|---|
| **Anything else?** | Ada apa lagi? |
| **That's it!** | Itu aju! |

| | |
|---|---|
| **Can I get some more [plain rice]?** | Minta [nasi putih] lagi? |
| **Do you like it?** | Suka? |
| **I like spicy food.** | Saya suka makanan yang pedas. |
| **I don't like salty food.** | Saya nggak suka makanan yang asin. |
| **This is absolutely delicious!** | Énak banget ini! |
| **This isn't very nice.** | Ini nggak énak. |
| **This isn't cooked through.** | Ini belum matang. |
| **This is still raw.** | Ini masih mentah. |
| **Have some more!** | Tambah lagi! |
| **I'm already full!** | Udah kenyang! |
| **Can I get the bill?** | Minta billnya? |

The correct word for "bill" in Indonesian is **bon**, but the English loanword, *bill*, is becoming increasingly ubiquitous. If you're trying to catch a waiter's eye across a crowded restaurant, the Indonesian sign-language for "bill" is to draw a little square in the air with the tips of both index fingers.

## HAND TO MOUTH

The usual way of eating in Indonesia is with a fork and a spoon, and this is what you'll get with your meal outside of tourist areas and posh restaurants. You hold the fork in your left hand and use it to shovel the food onto the spoon, which you hold in your right hand and use to transfer the food to your mouth. If you struggle with this you could try asking for a knife—**Minta pisau**—but in a basic eatery, chances are you'll be presented with a kitchen knife. Indonesians also often eat with their right hand—especially when eating steamed rice with chunks of fried meat or fish. At stalls selling this sort of thing you'll usually be provided with a bowl of warm water for washing your fingers before and after eating, but you can always ask for a fork and spoon—**Minta garpu séndok…**

## DRINKS & DRINKING

| | |
|---|---|
| **What do you want to drink?** | Mau minum apa? |
| **juice** | jus |
| **tea** | téh |
| **hot tea** | téh hangat |
| **iced tea** | es téh |
| **sweet tea** | téh manis |

| | |
|---|---|
| **unsweetened tea** | téh tawar |
| **coffee** | kopi |
| **coffee with milk** | kopi susu |
| **drinking water** | air putih |
| **don't use ice** | jangan pakai es |
| **beer** | bir |
| **alcohol** | alkohol/minuman keras (literally "hard drink", often abbreviated to **miras**) |
| **I don't drink alcohol.** | Saya nggak minum alkohol. |
| **I'm drunk!** | Saya mabuk! |

## ALCOHOL IN INDONESIA

Alcohol is fairly widely available in Indonesia, and although there are some very conservative areas of Sumatra where it can be tough to find an alcoholic drink, in most cities you shouldn't have too much trouble. Outside of high-end nightclubs and restaurants bottled beer (Bintang and Anker are the most popular local brands) is the commonest alcoholic beverage. In Bali and other eastern regions there are also some fierce local moonshine liquors, such as **arak**.

These are best avoided as they are sometimes tainted with ethanol and can cause serious illness or even blindness or death.

Overall, in Indonesia drinking alcohol is by no means the absolute social taboo that it is in many parts of the Middle East, but public drunkenness is very much frowned upon, as is conspicuous public alcohol consumption outside of designated bars and clubs.

## NGOPI

Indonesia has a serious café culture, with the cafés in question ranging from side-of-the-road stands to New York-style hipster coffee shops. And there's a great slang verb meaning "to go for a coffee"—**ngopi**…

# 8

# Hitting the Shops

## Buying and Bargaining

**SAYA & ANDA** (formal pronouns throughout)

**Let's go shopping!**     Yuk belanja!

Yuk is a more colloquial version of the word **ayo**, "let's go".
The final **k** is particularly subtle in this word, and the **u** is
foreshortened, so it ends up sounding very close to **ayo**
with the first syllable chopped off…

**I want to go to the mall.** Mau ke mal.

**shop**                    toko

**market**                  pasar

**I want to buy…**          Mau beli…

| | |
|---|---|
| **I want to sell…** | Mau jual… |
| **pay** | bayar |
| **money** | uang/duit |
| **I haven't got any cash!** | Nggak punya duit! |

## SLANG ALERT: Duit/uang="money"

**Uang** means "money"; **duit** is a slang term meaning something along the lines of "cash".

| | |
|---|---|
| **Where can I change currency?** | Dimana bisa tukar uang? |
| **What's the exchange rate?** | Apa kursnya? |
| **How many rupiah do I get?** | Dapat berapa rupiah? |
| **Is there an ATM near here?** | Ada ATM *(a-té-ém)* dekat sini? |
| **Can I pay with a credit card?** | Bisa pakai kartu kredit? |

**CHANGING MONEY**

In upscale shopping malls you can generally pay by credit cards, but for the most part Indonesia is still a cash economy. ATMs are easy to find, and most accept international credit and debit cards. You'll find them in banks, and also inside many convenience stores and malls. If you're dealing entirely in cash you'll find reliable money changers inside the biggest malls in major cities like Jakarta and Surabaya. In major tourist destinations there are lots of street-side exchange counters, but it's worth being careful with these; in Bali especially they have a reputation for shortchanging customers, so stick instead to exchange counters in banks and large licensed exchange offices.

## IN THE SHOPS

| | |
|---|---|
| **Can I help you?** | Bisa dibantu? |

This is another example of how Indonesians use the passive voice to be polite. **Bisa dibantu?** literally means "Can be helped?" A staff member could also say **Bisa saya bantu?** ("Can I help?"), or even **Bisa saya membantu anda?** ("Can I help you?"), but it is a bit too direct and forceful to use the active voice and the pronouns in this way.

| | |
|---|---|
| **What are you looking for?** | Cari apa? |
| **[I'm] just looking.** | Lihat-lihat aja. |
| **I'm looking for...** | Cari... |

**Lihat** means "look" as in "to look *at* something"; **cari** means "search" as in "to search *for* something".

| | |
|---|---|
| **I'm looking for something cheap.** | Cari sesuatu yang murah. |
| **... not expensive** | ... yang nggak mahal |
| **... distinctive** | ... yang unik |
| **... a gift for my [boyfriend/girlfriend]** | ... hadiah buat [pacar] saya |
| **... souvenirs** | ... oléh-oléh |
| **... a new one** | ... yang baru |
| **Can I have a look at that one?** | Coba lihat yang itu? |

**Coba** means "try", but **coba lihat** means "have a look" at something.

| | |
|---|---|
| **good** | baik |
| **excellent** | bagus |
| **ugly** | jelék |
| **bad** | buruk |

| | |
|---|---|
| **This one is better than that one!** | Ini lebih bagus daripada itu! |
| **They're exactly the same!** | Sama aja kok! |

## COLORS & SIZES

| | |
|---|---|
| **Do you have another color?** | Ada warna lain? |
| **Have you got it in red?** | Ada yang mérah? |
| **blue** | biru |
| **green** | hijau |
| **yellow** | kuning |
| **black** | hitam |
| **white** | putih |
| **gray** | abu-abu |
| **purple** | ungu |
| **brown** | coklat |
| **orange** | jingga |
| **pink** | merah muda |

**Merah muda** literally translates to "young red", which means pink. With other colors **muda** can be used to mean "light", while **tua** (lit., "old") can be used to mean "dark". **Hijau muda** is "light green" and **biru tua** is "dark blue".

| | |
|---|---|
| **This one is too big.** | Ini terlalu besar. |
| **Do you have a smaller size?** | Ada ukuran lebih kecil? |
| **big** | besar |
| **small** | kecil |
| **medium size** | ukuruan sedang |
| **extra large** | ekstra besar |
| **too small** | terlalu kecil |
| **not big enough** | kurang besar |

## DARIPADA
**Daripada** is used to compare something as "more" or "less" than something else. **Inggris lebih kecil daripada Indonesia** means "Britain is smaller than Indonesia".

## MANA OLÉH-OLÉHNYA?

The most important part of a traditional Indonesian holiday is the trip to buy **oléh-oléh**. This term is usually translated as "souvenirs", but it really means souvenirs to be given as gifts after returning home. If you're an Indonesian and you've been on holiday—even a quick weekend break— you're pretty much obliged to bring back a bunch of little gifts for friends, family members and colleagues. Favorite **oléh-oléh** items are keyrings, fridge magnets, and local dry snacks and biscuits. If you don't bring any gifts back with you you'll likely be met with an outraged **Mana oléh- oléhnya?** "Where are the souvenirs?"

A souvenir not specifically meant as a gift is a **kenang- kenangan** (this comes from the word **kenang**, "to recall", so is probably best translated as "keepsake") or a **cen- deramata** (this word is not commonly used, and it often implies a more substantial and high-quality souvenir).

## PRICES & BARGAINING

| How much is it? | Berapa harganya? |
|---|---|
| How much is this one? | Yang ini berapa harga? |
| How much is that one over there? | Berapa harga yang itu sana? |
| The price is … rupiah | Harganya … rupiah |

**Woah! So expensive!**     Loh! Mahal banget!

Loh is a word used to express shock or surprise.

**Too expensive**          Terlalu mahal

**No, it's not! It's cheap!**     Murah kok!

**Is that a fixed price?**     Itu harga pas atau nggak?

**Can it be discounted a bit?**     Bisa didiskon sedikit?

**To bargain**             Tawar-menawar

**Can we bargain?**        Bisa tawar-menawar?

**How much do you want to pay?**     Mau bayar berapa?

This is usually the question a vendor will use to open a round of bargaining after you've rejected their initial price. If you really want to throw yourself into the good-natured combat then there's absolutely no need to name your price at this stage; you could instead push them to come up with a lower initial asking price first.

**I don't know, but I don't want to pay that much!**
(lit., as much as that)

Nggak tahu, tapi nggak mahal segitu!

**Segitu** means "as that", from **itu** ("that"). You can also use **se** prefix to create other "as… as" constructs, e.g., **Sebesar itu** ("As big as that").

| | |
|---|---|
| **Can you reduce the price a bit?** | Bisa dikurangi sedikit? |
| **Reduce it more!** | Kurangi lagi dong! |
| **I can't. I'd make a loss.** | Nggak bisa. Saya rugi. |

**Rugi** ("make a loss") is a word much deployed by canny salesmen, trying to play on your conscience.

| | |
|---|---|
| **This is my last price.** | Ini harga terakhir. |
| **Give [five thousand] more!** | Kasih [lima ribu] lagi! |
| **Just reduce it by [five thousand] more!** | Kurangi [lima ribu] lagi aja! |
| **Ok, that's it; I don't want it if it's like that.** | Ya udah, nggak mau kalau begitu. |

## SLANG ALERT: Dong!

**Dong**—sometimes spelt **donk**, or in cutesy social media messages "*doank*"—is a slang term to create an imperative. It goes at the end of a sentence. **Duduk aja dong!** would mean something along the lines of "Just sit down, would you!"

## STRIKING A BARGAIN

Although prices in supermarkets, minimarts, and malls are generally fixed, Indonesia does have a long tradition of bargaining in its markets. You'll read all sorts of supposedly authoritative explanations of "how to bargain" in guidebooks, with one of the commonest assertions being that you should "aim to pay half the original asking price". In fact it's impossible to generalize like this. If you're buying everyday items in a non-tourist market, you might only reasonably expect a small discount of a few thousand rupiah; but if you're looking at mass-market handicrafts in a tourist hotspot the initial asking price could easily be ten times the true value of the item! If you're souvenir shopping the best bet is to first check out the prices in fixed-price emporiums—which you'll find in Bali, Yogyakarta, and most other major tourist destinations. Browsing the stock and checking out the price tags in these places is the best way to get a sense of what things are really worth.

## MONEY TALKS

The Indonesian currency is the rupiah. It comes in various denominations, both **uang kertas** ("paper money") and **koin** ("coins"). Exchange rates fluctuate wildly from year to year, but as a general rule of thumb when trying to get your head around the huge numbers involved it usually helps to think of Rp10,000 as being roughly equivalent to US$1.

| | |
|---|---|
| **Can you wrap it up for me?** | **Bisa dibungkus?** |
| **Can I have a receipt?** | **Minta kwitansi?** |

**I bought this here yesterday**      Ini saya beli disini kemarin

**Can I return it?**      Bisa dikembaliin?

## SLANG ALERT: Di...in/di...kan

To create the passive voice in Indonesian you generally
add the **di-** prefix to a word, sometimes also adding the
-kan suffix. **Kembali** is "return"; **dikembalikan** is "to be
returned". In colloquial Indonesian, however, the -kan
suffix is replaced with another suffix: **-in**. There's no need
to use this variation yourself, but you will hear other
people doing it, with **dikembalikan** becoming
**dikembaliin**.

# 9

# Tech Talk

## Phones, Computers and Social Media

**AKU & KAMU** (familiar pronouns throughout)

### ON THE PHONE

**hello** (on the phone)     halo

**Who is this?**     Ini dari siapa?

You can simply say **Ini siapa?** ("Who's this?"), but on the phone Indonesians tend to say **Ini dari siapa?** (literally "This is *from* who?").

**It's [John]!**     Ini [John]!

**Where are you?**     Kamu dimana?

| | |
|---|---|
| **I'm at home.** | **Aku di rumah.** |
| **Who with?** | **Sama siapa?** |
| **On my own.** | **Sama sendiri.** |

Indonesia, as a country where relatively few people had domestic landlines, adopted mobile telephony early—and with great gusto. Today mobile phones, most of them with data access, are utterly ubiquitous, and they come with a language all of their own. You can buy prepaid SIM cards (**kartu SIM**), including those with prepaid data, from phone shops and kiosks. These can be topped up with credit, which is available from the same shops and kiosks.

| | |
|---|---|
| **mobile phone** | **ponsél/HP** (pronounced *hé-pé*) |

**Ponsél** is short for **télépon sélular**, which doesn't need much translation, but colloquially a mobile phone is usually called a "HP". This is actually an abbreviation of an English loanword: "handphone".

| | |
|---|---|
| **phone credit** | **pulsa** |
| **I've run out of credit!** | **Pulsaku habis!** |
| **I want to buy some credit.** | **Mau beli pulsa.** |
| **Where can I get credit?** | **Dimana bisa dapat pulsa?** |
| **What's your cellphone number?** | **Apa nomor HPmu?** |

I want to buy some phone credit. **Mau beli pulsa.**

| | |
|---|---|
| **I'll give you a missed call.** | Aku missed-call dulu, ya. |
| **Did you get it (the number)?** | Masuk nggak? |
| **Got it!** | Masuk! (lit., "entered") |
| **text message** | SMS (pronounced as in English, *és-ém-és*) |
| **texting** | SMSan |
| **Text me!** | SMS aku! |

### MINTA PULSA DONG!

Most Indonesians use pay-as-you-go cellphones, and buy top-up credit as needed. You can **isi pulsa** ("fill up credit") at some ATMs and minimarts, but most people still get it from roadside kiosks where the vendor will top it up for you on the spot. You'll need to tell them which mobile network you use. The quest for **pulsa** is an endless one in this phone-addicted country, and many a parent complains that their teenage son or daughter tends to **makan pulsa** (literally "eats credit"). Pestering friends, and even distant acquaintances, for **pulsa** when you're short on cash is a national bad habit (anyone can top up your **pulsa** remotely, if you give them your number)—as is the annoying habit of the "missed call" (the English term is used in Indonesia). Want to speak to someone but don't have enough credit? "Missed-call" them, and hope they'll call you back!

## COMPUTERS & SOCIAL MEDIA

Most computer-related words in Indonesian have been borrowed from English. Remember that there is sometimes a spelling change—"computer" becomes **komputer**—and that on other occasions there's no change of spelling but there is a shift of pronunciation. The long Indonesian vowels in Wi-Fi make it sound like "wee-fee".

Indonesia is also a social-media obsessed country. The names of various networks are often abbreviated in Indonesian. Facebook is "FB" (pronounced éf-bé), and "Facebooking" is FBan. Instagram is hugely popular amongst Indonesians, and the country has one of the greatest concentrations of Twitter users on earth. But some networks that are hugely popular elsewhere, such as Snapchat and WhatsApp, don't have that much of a footprint, while others that are less well-known internationally are massive in Indonesia, Path for example.

New networks and new abbreviations are forever popping up, as old ones fade away—not too many people these days use *yé-ém* or *bé-bé-ém* (Yahoo Messenger and BlackBerry Messenger).

| | |
|---|---|
| **Are you on Facebook?** | Kamu punya FB? |
| | Kamu ada di FB? |
| **Is there Wi-Fi here?** | Ada Wi-Fi disini? |
| **Do you know where I can get free Wi-Fi?** | Tahu dimana ada Wi-Fi bébas? |
| **What's the password?** | Apa kata sandinya? |
| **What's the Wi-Fi key?** | Apa key Wi-Finya? |

The English loan-phrase *key Wi-Fi* is often used, with key pronounced as in English; the term **kode Wi-Fi** ("Wi-Fi code") is also used.

| | |
|---|---|
| **There's a problem with my connection.** | Konéksiku gagal. |
| **I'm chatting.** | Aku lagi chatting. |
| **Just send an email.** | Kirim email aja. |
| **Don't post this on Facebook, OK!** | Jangan posting di FB, ya! |
| **Take a selfie!** | Selfie dong! |

**Take a selfie with me!**     Selfie sama aku!

The word "selfie" has entered the Indonesian language, spelt and pronounced as in English. It is used as both a noun and a verb. In fact, it's even developed a full formal verb form, with the **ber-** prefix: **berselfie**.

## TEXT-SPEAK

Social media is the frontline when it comes to ultra-colloquial Indonesian. And the digital version of the language is not only seriously slang-laden and disengaged from normal grammar rules; it also tends towards extreme abbreviations. Words get pared down to within an inch of their lives, and what's more some Indonesians (those mocked by their more sophisticated peers for being **Alay** or "Over the top") like to swap letters for numbers and to let emoticons do all the heavy lifting of the syntax. Disentangling meanings from the most extreme text-speak can be tricky even for those with excellent language skills, but we'll show you a few of the more straightforward abbreviations you might find in a text message or Facebook post here.

| aj | aja | just, only |
|---|---|---|
| bhs | bahasa | language |
| bpk | bapak | sir, father |
| brngkt | berangkat | leave |
| bru | baru | new, just now |
| bs | bisa | can |
| byk | banyak | lots |
| cew | céwék | girl |
| cpt | cepat | fast, quickly |
| dlm | dalam | in |
| dgn | dengan | with |
| dmn | dimana | where |
| dr | dari | from |
| emg | emang | indeed/for sure |
| knp | kenapa | why |
| kt | kita | we |
| m | sama | with/together |
| q | aku | I |
| qm | kamu | you |
| sm | sama | same, with |
| td | tadi | earlier |
| x | kali | times |
| yg | yang | that which is the… one |

# 10

# Getting Social

## Chitchat, Small talk and Emotions

**AKU & KAMU** (familiar pronouns throughout)

| | |
|---|---|
| **I want to chat with you guys.** | Aku péngén ngobrol sama kalian. |
| **What are you guys talking about?** | Kalian ngobrol tentang apa saja? |
| **Join us!** | Mampir dong! |

**Mampir** literally means "drop in" or "stop by", and someone might invite you to **mampir ke rumah**, "to drop in at the house". But it's also used if you happen to be passing a group of people sitting around and they cheerfully call you to sit down and join them there and then. This is a fairly frequent occurrence especially if you can speak a bit of Indonesian, and may also happen if you pass a group of friends at a café or food court.

**Hey! It's lively here at the moment!**    Eh! Ramé disini sekarang!

**Ramé** is correctly spelt **ramai**, but the final syllable is often pronounced as an é colloquially. "Busy" doesn't usually have the negative connotations it can take on in English, and when someone says a place is **ramé** they're usually speaking approvingly. It might be better thought of as meaning "lively".

**I've got some gossip from work!**    Ada gosip dari kantor!

**Did you hear about it?**    Kamu udah denger belum?

**... and then he/she said...**    ... terus dia bilang...

**... and after that I said...**    ... habis itu aku bilang...

**What do you think?**    Apa pikiranmu?

**What a pity!**    Kasihan!

**Kasihan** means "pity", but it can also mean "feel sorry for". **Kasihan kamu** means "poor you". It's usually said in seriousness, but it can also be said in playful mockery, meaning something like "Ha! Bad luck!" This is particularly in the case of the pop culture catchphrase **Kasihan deh lu** (which uses **lu**, the Jakarta-slang equivalent of **kamu**).

**I don't care**
**[about him/her].**

Aku nggak peduli
[sama dia].

**It's not important!**    Nggak penting!

The phrase **nggak penting** means a lot more than its directly translated equivalent. It can be said—with a tone ranging from mild to extreme annoyance—to dismiss any topic which you consider to be a pointless waste of time, or any activity or person that inspires the same response. If you're being stupid, not taking things seriously or wasting a friend's time, they might say **Ah, nggak penting kamu!** It translates as "You're not important", but really means "You're being really annoying!" A similar English equivalent might be the dismissive "Whatever!"

**It's definitely like that.**    Iya emang kayak gitu.

**Tell me!**    Kasihtau!

**Wouldn't you like**
**to know!**

Mau tahu aja!

This is a playful way of responding when someone's asking about something you don't want to share. It can be used with real force and annoyance, but usually it's just part of friendly backchat.

**That's nonsense.**    Itu omong kosong.
(literally "empty talk")

**You're lying!**    Bohong kamu!

| | |
|---|---|
| **Bullshit!** | **Bulsyit!** |

This is an English loanword that's become increasingly common.

| | |
|---|---|
| **I'm just messing with you!** | **Iseng aja!** |

| | |
|---|---|
| **I'm only joking** | **Aku cuman bercanda** |

| | |
|---|---|
| **You think you're so funny!** | **Jayus kamu!** |

**Jayus** is a brilliant slang term, meaning something roughly along the lines of "something intended to be funny, which really isn't". You can use it to describe both a cheesy joke—and the person who makes the cheesy jokes!

| | |
|---|---|
| **You're a know it all!** | **Sok tahu kamu!** |

## SLANG ALERT: Denger/dengar="hear"

**Dengar**, "hear", is properly spelt with an "a" in the last syllable, but it's one of those words where this sound often turns into a short "e" in colloquial Indonesian: **denger**.

## PUT A SOK IN IT!

**Sok** is a slang term meaning literally "pretend", so when someone says you're **sok tahu** they're literally saying you "pretend to know"—i.e., that you think you know what you're talking about, but you really don't. **Sok tahu** is the phrase you're most likely to come across, but it crops up elsewhere too. If someone's said to be **sok kaya** it's a particularly biting comment. It literally means "pretend rich" and is used to talk about someone who makes out like he's a wealthy big shot, but really isn't.

## FEELINGS & EMOTIONS

| | |
|---|---|
| **What's up with you?** | Kamu kenapa? |
| **There's nothing up with me.** | Aku nggak apa-apa. |
| **I'm happy.** | Aku senang. |
| **I'm sad.** | Aku sedih. |
| **I'm in a bad mood.** | Aku bété. |

**Bété** was actually originally an abbreviation, "BT", but no one seems to remember what it originally meant! Theories range from a straightforward English borrowing, "Bad Tempered", to **Banyak Tekanan** ("lots of pressure") and **Bosan Total** ("totally bored"). The exact origin of many other words that make the crossover from Bahasa Gaul to mainstream Indonesian is similarly murky.

| | |
|---|---|
| **angry** | marah |
| **tired** | capék |
| **bored** | bosan |
| **This is so boring!** | Ini membosankan banget! |

| | |
|---|---|
| **scared** | takut |
| **lazy** | malas |
| **annoyed** | sebel/kesel |
| **annoying** | menyebalkan |
| **shocked** | kaget |
| **disappointed** | kecéwa |
| **worried** | cemas |
| **There's no need to worry.** | Nggak usah cemas. |
| **confused** | bingung |

| | |
|---|---|
| **Come on! Meet my friends!** | Ayo! Ketemu teman-temanku! |
| **I'm shy, you know!** | Aku malu tau! |

### DON'T BE SHY!

**Malu** is a much-used word, with various subtle differences of meaning. Depending on the context it can mean shy, embarrassed or ashamed. To all these emotions the response might be **Jangan malu** ("Don't be shy") or **Nggak usah malu** ("No need to be embarrassed"). Some indication of the core nature of the word is the fact that it provides the root for the term **kemaluan**, which ought to mean "shame", but which is actually a rather quaint euphemism for genitals (if you really want to talk about "shame", "embarrassment" or "shyness", then you should say **rasa malu**, literally "a feeling of **malu**"). Avoid using the literal translation of "my shame", or **Kemaluanku**, as it actually means "my genitals"!

| | |
|---|---|
| **Why are you sad?** | Kenapa kamu sedih? |
| **Because I just broke up with my boyfriend/ girlfriend!** | Gara-gara aku baru putus sama pacarku! |

**Baru** literally means "new", but it's also a way of saying "very recently", or "just now". In this usage you can also add **saja** to mean "just this instant", e.g., **Aku baru saja datang** (lit., "I've just this instant arrived").

| | |
|---|---|
| **Why are you melancholy again?** | Kenapa kamu mellow lagi? |

**Because I miss my boyfriend/girlfriend.**

**Karena aku kangen sama pacarku.**

Why are you sad?
**Kenapa kamu sedih?**

Because I just broke up with my girlfriend.
**Gara-gara aku baru putus sama pacarku.**

## SLANG ALERT: Mellow Yellow

If your Indonesian friend seems to be looking a bit miserable, they might tell you **Aku mellow**—which sounds odd to an English speaker, but that's because **mellow** means something quite different in Indonesian from its more positive English inference. **Mellow** is the sort of melancholy state you might be in while pining over an unrequited love.

The actual English word "mellow", meanwhile, to describe a character or atmosphere, doesn't translate very easily into Indonesian, but words like **lembut** or **empuk** ("soft" or "tender") come close to the same meaning when talking about flavours or sensations.

**SLANG ALERT:**
# Gara-gara/karena="because"

The usual way to say "because" in Indonesian is **karena**, but you'll sometimes hear people speaking colloquially using the term **gara-gara** instead. The two are totally interchangeable.

# 11

# Dating, Mating, Hating

## Love, Sex, Break-ups and Insults

**AKU & KAMU** (familiar pronouns throughout)

### DATING

| | |
|---|---|
| **dating someone** | pacaran |
| **boyfriend/girlfriend** | pacar |
| **partner** | jodoh |

**Jodoh** means partner in the intimate sense, but it also conveys the idea of a "good match"; your **jodoh** is probably "The One". **Menjodohkan** means "To set someone up with someone"; **dijodohkan** is "to be set up with someone".

| | |
|---|---|
| **love** (noun) | **percintaan** |
| **love** (verb) | **cinta** |

## DATING, INDONESIAN STYLE

Phrasebooks tend to list all sorts of cheesy chat-up lines (usually in hilariously inappropriate formal language) and forthright invitations to take things to the next level within minutes of meeting. In real life dating is an essential part of life for Indonesians, but it usually starts in gentle fashion, with a process called **pendekatan** "getting close", or colloquially known as PDKT or **pédékaté**. You meet someone in a social context, through friends, at work or school—or maybe just hanging out as fellow travelers while on a backpacking trip—and you start to "get close"; then you go on a few dates, and they become your **pacar**—the unisex Indonesian word for boyfriend/girlfriend. If you're just passing through as a traveler you could always ask someone you meet out on a date, but don't necessarily expect things to move as quickly as they might back home. Instead, it might be better to get their contact number and build up a friendship first.

| | |
|---|---|
| **Do you want [to go to the movies] with me tomorrow?** | Mau [ke bioskop] sama aku bésok? |
| **Do you want to go out with me tomorrow evening?** | Mau jalan-jalan sama aku bésok malam? |

| | |
|---|---|
| I'll pick you up at [six o'clock]. | Aku jemputmu [jam enam]. |
| I'm having a good time here with you. | Aku senang disini sama kamu. |
| I want to go home. | Aku mau pulang. |
| Do you want to come home with me? | Mau pulang sama aku? |
| Do you want to come back to my place? | Mau pulang ke tempatku? |
| No way! I want to go home on my own! | Nggak-lah! Mau pulang sendiri! |

The **-lah** suffix is sometimes tagged onto yes and no to give them extra force; **Nggak-lah!** is "No way!" To be particularly forceful with the positive equivalent, you double the **ya: Iya-ya-lah!**

| | |
|---|---|
| I'm not a chicken, you know! | Aku bukan ayam tau! |

**Ayam** ("chicken") in this context is a pejorative word for a "woman of loose morals". It doesn't quite mean prostitute, but something very close to that ("prostitute" is **pelacur**).

| | |
|---|---|
| I already have a boyfriend/girlfriend. | Aku udah punya pacar. |
| I'm still single. | Aku masih jomblo. |

| | |
|---|---|
| **I like you.** | Aku suka sama kamu. |
| **You're funny.** | Kamu lucu. |
| **I want to get closer to you.** | Aku mau lebih dekat sama kamu. |
| **Do you want to go out with me?** | Mau pacaran sama aku? |
| **Do you want to be my boyfriend/girlfriend?** | Mau jadi pacarku? |

**Jadi** means "become" in this instance, but it can also mean "so" or "therefore".

| | |
|---|---|
| **He/she cheated on me so I asked to break up!** | Dia selingkuh, jadi aku mintu putus! |

## SWEET WORDS

| | |
|---|---|
| **You're pretty.** | Kamu cantik. |

**Cantik** and **indah** both mean "pretty" or "beautiful". **Cantik** can be applied to both a girl, and a thing; **indah** can only be applied to a thing, most typically a place or a landscape, though it can also describe an abstractly beautiful situation.

| | |
|---|---|
| **You're handsome.** | Kamu cakap. |
| **You're sweet.** | Kamu manis. (really only appropriate when addressing a girl) |

| | |
|---|---|
| **You're so kind.** | Kamu baik hati sekali. |
| **Your eyes are beautiful.** | Matamu cantik. |
| **lips** | bibir |
| **cheeks** | pipi |
| **body** | badan |
| **You're so sexy.** | Kamu séksi banget. |
| **I love you!** | Aku cinta sama kamu! <br> Aku sayang sama kamu! |
| **You're everything to me!** | Kamu segalanya bagi aku! |
| **Do you love me?** | Sayang sama aku nggak? |
| **my love** | sayangku |
| **darling** | kekasih |
| **I miss you.** | Aku kangen samu kamu. |

**SLANG ALERT: Cakap/ganteng**

Ganteng means "handsome"; cakap is a slightly more slangy way to say that a man is good-looking.

## SLANG ALERT: **Kangen/rindu**

The formal Indonesian word for "miss" or "yearn" is **rindu**, and you can certainly use it to say you miss someone: **Aku merindukanmu** or **Aku rindu sama kamu**. It can also become a noun: **Rinduku pada kamu** is "My yearning for you". Colloquially, however, you're more likely to hear the word **kangen**. You can say **Aku kangen sama kamu/sama John** ("I miss you/John"), but you can also simply say **Aku kangen** ("I feel longing"), to which the response might be **Sama siapa?** ("For who?"). Unlike **rindu, kangen** doesn't work as a noun on its own, but you can talk about **rasa kangen**, "a feeling of longing".

## SAYANGKU!

**Sayang** is a multipurpose word. It can mean "unfortunately", especially when tagged onto **-nya** or paired with **sekali** ("very"). **Sayangnya/sayang sekali, kita tidak bisa** means "Unfortunately, we couldn't do it". But **sayang** also means "love", as both a verb and a noun: you can say you are **sayang** with someone, meaning you love them, or you can say they are your **sayang**, your "love", or your "darling". The connection between love and misfortune might not seem to make much sense, but perhaps **sayang** is best translated as "dear". You might call someone "my dear", say they are "dear to you", but you might also say "oh dear!" if you hear of bad news…

## IN THE BEDROOM

| | |
|---|---|
| I want to kiss you. | Aku mau cium kamu. |
| Kiss me! | Cium aku! |
| Hug me! | Peluk aku! |
| Take this off (clothes). | Lepas ini. |
| Close your eyes. | Tutup matamu. |
| Do you want to make love? | Mau bercinta? |

**Bercinta** is probably the nicest way to say "to have sex". It's certainly more romantic than **berhubungan séks**, which is roughly equivalent to "have sexual intercourse". **Séks** is sometimes used on its own, but it sounds slightly coarse, as does the very slangy **ngséx**. Even coarser—to the point of being very offensive—are words for sex like **ngéwek** and **ngentot**.

| | |
|---|---|
| Does it feel good like this? | Énak kalau begini? |
| Stop! I don't want it. | Jangan! Aku nggak mau. |
| It doesn't feel good. | Nggak énak. |
| Use a condom. | Pakai kondom. |

## TAKING THE NEXT STEP

| | |
|---|---|
| **Are you serious about me?** | Kamu sérius sama aku? |
| **Do you want to meet my parents?** | Mau ketemu orangtuaku? |
| **Will you marry me?** | Mau menikah sama aku? |
| **Do you want to be my wife/husband?** | Mau jadi istriku/suamiku? |
| **I got you a ring.** | Aku dapat cincin buat kamu. |
| **fiancé** | calon suami |
| **fiancée** | calon istri |

You can also use the unisex term **tunangan** for fiancé/fiancée.

| | |
|---|---|
| **When will we get married?** | Kapan kita menikah? |
| **Just when are we going to get married?** | Kapan saja kita menikah? |
| **You promised!** | Kamu udah janji! |
| **I'm running out of patience!** | Aku nggak sabar lagi! |

## BREAKING IT OFF

| | |
|---|---|
| **I want to break up [with you].** | Aku mau putus [sama kamu]. |
| **I don't want to be with you any more.** | Aku nggak mau sama kamu lagi. |
| **Why do you want to break up?** | Kenapa mau putus? |
| **You're mean to me.** | Kamu jahat sama aku. |
| **I know you've cheated on me.** | Aku tau kamu pernah selingkuh. |
| **You can't be faithful.** | Kamu nggak bisa setia. |
| **You're not romantic!** | Kamu nggak romantis! |
| **You're uncaring.** | Kamu cuék. |
| **You're so self-centered.** | Kamu égois banget. |
| **You're cruel.** | Kamu sadis. |

**Sadis** comes from "sadistic", so it means really cruel!

| | |
|---|---|
| **I feel like you don't love me anymore.** | Aku merasa kamu nggak sayang lagi sama aku. |
| **It seems like you don't respect me.** | Kayaknya aku nggak dihargai kamu. |

| | |
|---|---|
| **We're not well-matched.** | Kita nggak cocok. |

Cocok means "well-matched" or "suitable". It can refer to a romantic partner, but it can also refer to an item of clothing, a color scheme for a house, or any number of other things. You could ask **Baju ini cocok nggak?** ("Does this shirt suit me?") or you could ask your friends **Pacar baruku cocok sama aku nggak?** ("Is my new boyfriend/girlfriend a good match for me?")

| | |
|---|---|
| **broken hearted** | sakit hati/patah hati |
| **I have another boyfriend/girlfriend.** | Aku punya pacar lain. |
| **You playboy!** | Kamu buaya! |
| **Typical playboy!** | Dasar cowok buaya darat! |

**Buaya** means "crocodile", but **buaya darat**, "land crocodile", is a playboy, a guy who messes around with girls' hearts. **Buaya** can only be used to describe a man.

## CURSES & INSULTS

If a break-up turns nasty you might find yourself using harsh words, so we've listed a few insults here—none of which are exclusively for use when fighting with a former lover!

Indonesia has a rich array of swearwords, but many of them are specifically regional slang, used in one city or province and little known elsewhere, while others are buried deep in lower levels of Bahasa Gaul and would mean nothing to the average person. What Indonesia doesn't really have is the small collection of ubiquitous, all-purpose swearwords that appear in English—perhaps because Indonesians are more imaginative with their cursing!

Using curses in a language that's not your own mother tongue is almost never a good idea, even if you speak it fluently. You'll usually sound ridiculous (like a non-native speaker clumsily trying to use the F-word in English), or end up being far more offensive than you intended. The words and phrases below are included here for fun. We strongly recommend that you don't ever actually use them—other than in jest to amuse your close Indonesian friends!

| | |
|---|---|
| **I hate you!** | Aku benci sama kamu! |
| **You're stupid!** | Kamu bodoh! |
| **Typical idiot!** | Dasar bodoh! |
| **idiot** | goblok |

**Goblok** is actually a fairly strong word, roughly halfway between "idiot" and "fuck-wit"! Other relatively mild words for "idiot" include **tolol** and **dodol**.

| | |
|---|---|
| **Monkey!** | Monyét! |
| **You monkey!** | Monyét kamu! |

When using insults it's more common—and more force-ful—to place the pronoun after the insult itself: **Monyét kamu**, rather than **kamu monyét**.

| **jerk** | **brengsek** |
|---|---|

Many words like **brengsek** can be used as expressive curses (like saying "Shit!" or "Damn it!" in English) as well as direct personal insults.

## YOU MONKEY!

It's always worth remembering that words which seem to be fairly mild in direct translation might actually pack a good deal more punch in another language. Calling someone **monyét** ("monkey"), **anjing** ("dog") or **babi** ("pig") in Indonesian is a lot more aggressive and offensive than it would in English, something like "asshole". As for the word **bajingan**, which comes from **bajing** ("squirrel") and so should literally mean something equivalent to "squirrelly" or "squirrel-ness"—it's actually a really strong insult, something along the lines of "bastard" or "scumbag"!

| **Piss off!** | **Matamu!** |
|---|---|

**Matamu** literally means "your eyes", but saying it with force turns it into an insult. Sometimes people place an expletive up front to add further insult. In Surabaya, East Java, the exceptionally offensive local dialect word **jancok** gets used this way: **Jancok matamu** is basically a really nasty way to say "Fuck off!" Don't ever say it to anyone in Surabaya though, unless you're looking for a fight—the city has a reputation for hot tempers!

**female genitalia**          mémék

**male genitalia**           kontol

These are very crude words—you can work out your own English-language equivalents! And just as in English, they can be directed at a person as an insult.

**shit**                      tahi

**Tahi**—which typically loses the "h" in speech to become **tai**—is stronger than its English equivalent, especially when you use it directly towards a person: **Tahi kamu!** is a very strong insult. It's stronger still if you call someone **tahi kucing**—literally "cat shit".

**fuck**                      ngentot

There are various Indonesian and regional dialect words that could be translated as "fuck", but this is probably the commonest, and the one closest to its English equivalent. It is both a crude verb meaning "to have sex", an expressive curse ("Fuck!"), and a direct insult (**Ngentot kamu!** "Fuck you!"). Inevitably, the English word itself has also crept into colloquial Indonesian, though the pronunciation tends to nudge the **f** towards becoming **p**: "*Puk yu!*"

# English–Indonesian Dictionary

Verbs are listed in their root form, which can generally be used in place of the full verb in colloquial Indonesian. Words are identified as "v" (verb), "n" (noun" or "a" (adjective) where necessary for clarity.

**A**

able, to be **bisa**
about (around, approximately) **kira-kira**
about (regarding) **tentang**
above, upstairs **di atas**
accent **logat**
accident **kecelakaan**
accommodation **akomodasi, penginapan**
accurate **teliti**
active **giat**
activity **kegiatan**
add to **tambah**
address **alamat**
administration **administrasi**
admit, confess **akui**
adult **dewasa**
advance money **uang muka**
after **sesudah**
afternoon (3pm to dusk) **soré**
afternoon (midday) **siang**
age **umur, usia**
agree **setuju**
air **udara**
air-conditioning **AC** (this is an English loan, pronounced as in English)
airplane **pesawat**
airport **bandara**
alight (get off) **turun**
alcohol **alkohol, minuman keras**

all **semua**
allergy, allergic **alergi**
allow **biarkan**
all over **seluruh**
almost **hampir**
alone **sendiri**
already **sudah**
also **juga**
America **Amérika**
American (person) **(orang) Amérika**
among **antara**
amount **jumlah**
ancient **kuno**
and **dan**
angry **marah**
animal **binatang, héwan**
annoy **menjéngkélkan**
annoyed **sebal, kesel**
annoying **menyebalkan**
antiques **barang antik**
apart from **kecuali**
apartment **apartemen**
apple **apel**
appointment **janji**
approximately **kira-kira**
area **wilayah**
arm **lengan**
around **sekitar**
arrest **tangkap**
arrive **datang**
art **seni**
art gallery **galeri seni**

artist **pelukis**
ascend **naik**
ask; ask (a question) **tanya**
ask (for something) **minta**
aspirin **aspirin**
at night **pada malam hari**
Australia **Australia**
Australian **(orang) Australia**

**B**
baby **bayi**
babysitter **pengasuh anak**
back (of body) **punggung**
back (go) **balik**
back (rear) **belakang**
backpack **tas ransel**
backpacker **turis ransel**
bag **tas**
baggage **bagasi**
balcony **balkon**
bald **botak, gundul**
ball **bola**
banana **pisang**
bandage **perban**
bank (finance) **bank**
bank (river) **tepi**
bargain (v) **tawar-menawar**
basketball **(bola) basket**
bathe **mandi**
bathroom **kamar mandi**
battery **baterai**
beach **pantai**
beautiful **indah**
because **karena**
bed **tempat tidur**
bee **lebah**
beef **daging sapi**
beer **bir**
before **sebelum**
begin **mulai**

behind **belakang**
believe **percaya**
belt **sabuk**
beneath **bawah**
beside **samping, sebelah**
best **terbaik**
better **lebih baik**
between **antara**
bicycle **sepéda**
big, large **besar, gedé**
bigger **lehih besar**
biggest **terbesar**
bikini **bikini**
bill **bon, bil**
bird **burung** (also slang for penis)
birth **lahir**
birthday **ulang tahun**
bite **gigit**
bitter **pahit**
black **hitam**
blanket **selimut**
blood **darah**
blouse **blus**
blue **biru**
boat **perahu**
body **badan**
boil **rebus**
bone **tulang**
book **buku**
booked, reserved **sudah direservasi**
border **perbatasan**
bored **bosan**
boring **membosankan**
borrow **pinjam**
bottle **botol**
box **kotak**
boy (child) **anak laki-laki**
boyfriend/girlfriend **pacar**

brain **otak**
brave **berani**
bread **roti**
break off, break up **putus**
breakfast **sarapan**
breathe **nafas**
bribe **sogok**
bridge **jembatan**
bright (of light) **terang**
bring **bawa**
broken **patah, rusak, hancur**
brother **saudara**
brown **coklat**
bucket **émbér**
building **gedung**
burn **bakar**
bus **bis**
bus station **terminal (bis)**
bus stop **halté bis**
busy, lively (of a place) **ramai**
busy (of a person) **sibuk**
but **tetapi, tapi**
butter **mentéga**
buy **beli**
by airmail **pos udara**

**C**
café **kafe**
cake **kué**
call, name (v) **panggil**
calm **tenang**
camera **kamera**
camping **berkemah**
can (be able) **bisa, dapat,**
  **mampu**
canceled **batal**
cancer **kanker**
candidate **calon**
candle **lilin**
capsule (medicine) **kapsul**

car **mobil**
cardigan **baju hangat**
cash **uang tunai**
cash machine **mesin ATM**
cat **kucing**
cave **gua**
celebrate **merayakan**
center **pusat**
century **abad**
certain **yakin**
certainly **betul**
change (v) **ganti**
chair **kursi**
champagne **sampanye**
chaos, disorder **kacau**
cheap **murah**
check **periksa**
check in **lapor**
check out **keluar**
checked luggage **(koper)**
  **bagasi**
cheese **kéju**
chef **koki**
chicken **ayam**
child **anak**
chocolate **cokelat**
choose **pilih**
Christian **Kristen**
Christmas **Natal**
church **geréja**
cigarette **rokok**
cinema **bioskop**
citizen, member **warga**
city centre **pusat kota**
city **kota**
clean (a) **bersih**
clean (v) **membersihkan**
clear **jelas**
cliff **tebing**
climb **mendaki**

clock **jam**
close, closed **tutup**
close, near **dekat**
closest **terdekat**
closet **lemari**
cloth **kain**
clothes **pakaian, baju** (top, e.g., a sweater or t-shirt)
clothes dryer **mesin pengering baju**
clothes hanger **gantungan baju**
clown **badut**
coat **jas**
cockroach **kecoa**
cocoa **coklat**
coconut **kelapa**
coffee **kopi**
cold (temperature) **dingin**
cold (flu) **pilek, masuk angin**
collar **kerah**
colleague **rekan**
cologne **minyak wangi**
color **warna**
comb (n) **sisir**
come **datang**
come back **kembali**
comfortable **nyaman**
complaint **keluhan**
computer **komputer**
concert **konser**
condom **kondom**
confidence **percaya diri**
confirm **konfirmasi**
connection **hubungan**
cook (v) **masak**
cool, great **asyik**
corn **jagung**
corruption **korupsi**
count (v) **hitung**

country **negara**
cow **sapi**
crab **kepiting**
crash **tabrak**
crazy **gila**
credit **krédit, pulsa** (specifically phone credit)
crocodile **buaya**
culture **budaya**
curry **karé**
cut (a) **berluka**
cut (slice) **potong**
cut (wound) **luka**
cute **lucu**
cycle-rickshaw **bécak**

**D**

daily **harian**
dairy products **produk olahan susu**
damage **kerusakan**
dance **tari**
danger **bahaya**
dangerous **berbahaya**
dark **gelap**
date of birth **tanggal kelahiran**
daughter **anak perempuan**
dawn **dini hari**
day **hari**
day after tomorrow **lusa**
day before yesterday **kemarin dulu**
dead **mati**
deaf **tuli**
delayed **tertunda**
delicious **énak, lezat, gurih**
deodorant **deodoran**
depart **berangkat**
departure time **jam keberangkatan**

deposit (v) **menyetor**
descend **turun**
dessert **pencuci mulut**
destination **tujuan**
diarrhea **diaré**
dictionary **kamus**
die **meninggal**
diet **diet**
different **béda**
difficult **susah, sulit**
dining room **ruang makan**
dinner **makan malam**
direct **langsung**
direct flight **penerbangan lansung**
direct, straight **lurus**
direction **jurusan**
dirty **kotor**
disabled **cacat**
disco **disko**
distilled water **air suling**
disturb **ganggu**
dive (v) **menyelam**
diving (scuba) **selam scuba**
divorce **cerai**
dizzy **pusing**
do **melakukan**
doctor **dokter**
dog **anjing**
doll **boneka**
dolphin **lumba-lumba**
don't (imperative) **jangan**
door, gate **pintu**
doubt **ragu**
down **ke bawah**
dream (v) **mimpi**
dress **rok**
drink (alcoholic) **minuman keras**
drink (n) **minuman**

drink (v) **minum**
drinking water **air minum, air putih**
drive **mengemudi**
driver **pengemudi, sopir**
driver's licence **SIM**
drugs (illegal) **narkoba**
drugstore **apotik**
drunk **mabuk**
dry (a) **kering**
dry (v) **jemur**
dry-clean **cuci di binatu**
duck (n) **bébék**
dumb (mute) **bisu**
duty-free shop **toko bebas pajak**

**E**
each **setiap**
ear **telinga**
earlier, previously **tadi**
early **awal**
earrings **anting-anting**
earthenware **tembikar**
earthquake **gempa bumi**
east **timur**
easy **mudah, gampang**
eat **makan**
economical **hemat**
economy class **kelas ekonomi**
eczema **eksim**
education **pendidikan**
eel **belut**
egg **telur**
egotistical, self-centered **égois**
electric, electricity **listrik**
elephant **gajah**
elevator **lift**

email **imel**
embassy **kedutaan**
emergency brake **rem darurat**
emergency exit **pintu darurat**
emotional **émosi**
empty (*a*) **kosong**
end (*n*) **akhir**
engaged (to be married) **bertunangan**
engagement (appointment) **janji**
England, Great Britain, the United Kingdom **Inggris, Britania Raya**
English **Bahasa Inggris**
enjoy (*v*) **menikmati**
enjoy **bersenang-senang**
enough **cukup**
enter **masuk**
equipment **alat**
event **peristiwa**
every **setiap**
every day **setiap hari**
everyone **semua orang**
everything **semuanya**
everywhere **di mana-mana**
evidence **bukti**
exactly **persis**
example **contoh, misal**
excellent **baik sekali**
except **selain**
exchange office **kantor penukaran uang**
excuse, reason **alasan**
exit **pintu keluar**
expensive **mahal**
expert **ahli, juru**
explain **menjelaskan**
extraordinary **luar biasa**

eye **mata**

**F**
fabric **bahan**
face **muka**
factory **pabrik**
fail **gagal**
faint (*v*) **pingsan**
fall (*v*) **jatuh**
false **palsu**
family **keluarga**
famous **terkenal**
fan **kipas angin**
far, distance **jauh**
fare **ongkos**
farm **pertanian**
farmer **petani**
fashion **gaya**
fast **cepat**
fat **gemuk**
father **ayah**
father, mister **bapak**
father-in-law **bapak mertua**
fault **kesalahan**
feeling, flavor **rasa**
fever **deman**
fiancé, fiancée **tunangan**
fill (*v*) **isi**
film **film**
final **terakhir**
fine (money) **denda**
finger **jari**
finished, completed **selesai**
fire **api**
fire extinguisher **pemadam api**
first **pertama**
first aid **pertolongan pertama**
first class **kelas satu**

fish **ikan**
fitness club **tempat fitness**
fitting room **kamar pas**
fix, mend **memperbaiki**
flag **bendéra**
flashlight **lampu senter**
flavor **rasa**
flea market **pasar loak**
flee **kabut**
flood **banjir**
floor **lantai**
flower **bunga**
flu **pilek**
fluent **fasih, lancar**
fly (*n*) **lalat**
fly (*v*) **terbang**
follow **ikut**
following (the) **yang berikutnya**
food **makanan**
food poisoning **keracunan makanan**
food stall **warung**
foot, leg **kaki**
football **sepakbola**
for **untuk**
forbidden **dilarang**
foreign **asing**
foreigner **orang asing**
forest **hutan, rimba**
forever **selalu, untuk selamanya**
forget **lupa**
fork **garpu**
formal dress **pakaian resmi**
fort **bénténg**
France **Perancis**
French person **(orang) Perancis**
free (*adj*) **gratis, bébas**

fresh **segar**
Friday **Jumat**
fried **goréng**
friend **teman, kawan**
frog **kodok**
from **dari**
front **depan**
fruit **buah**
frustrated **frustrasi**
fry **goréng**
full (after eating) **kenyang**
full **penuh**
funny, cute **lucu**
future **masa depan**

**G**
gallery **galeri**
game **permainan**
garage (car repair) **bengkel**
garden **kebun**
garlic **bawang putih**
gas (heating) **gas**
gas station **pompa bensin**
gasoline **bensin**
gate **gerbang**
gay **gay, homo**
Germany **Jerman**
get off (vehicle) **turun**
get on (vehicle) **naik**
get up **bangun**
ghost **hantu**
gift **hadiah**
ginger **jahé**
girl (child) **anak perempuan**
girlfriend **pacar**
give **beri, kasih**
given name **nama depan**
glass (for drinking) **gelas**
glass **kaca**
glasses (spectacles) **kacamata**

glue **lem**
go back **kembali**
go home **pulang**
go **pergi**
goat **kambing**
god **tuhan**
gold **emas**
golf **golf**
golf course **lapangan golf**
good **baik, bagus**
good afternoon **selamat siang**
good evening, good night **selamat malam**
good morning **selamat pagi**
goodbye (to the person leaving) **selamat jalan**
goodbye (to the person remaining) **selamat tinggal**
goods, baggage **barang**
grandchild **cucu**
grandfather **kakék**
grandmother **nénék**
grass **rumput**
gray **abu-abu**
graze (injury) **luka lecet**
green **hijau**
gridlock **macet**
group **kelompok**
guarantee **garansi**
guess **taksir**
guest **tamu**
guesthouse **losmen**
gun **senjata**
gym **tempat fitnes**

## H

hair **rambut**
hairbrush **sikat rambut**
haircut **potong rambut**
hairdresser **penata rambut**
hairdryer **pengering rambut**
hairstyle **gaya rambut**
half **setengah**
hand **tangan**
hand luggage **bagasi kabin**
handbag **tas tangan**
handbrake **rem tangan**
handmade **buatan tangan**
handsome **ganteng**
happy **senang, gembira, bahagia**
harbor **pelabuhan**
hard (difficult) **sulit**
hard, loud **keras**
hat **topi**
hate **benci**
have **punya**
he, she **dia**
head **kepala**
headache **sakit kepala**
health **keséhatan**
healthy **séhat**
hear **dengar**
heat, hot **panas**
heavy (weight) **berat**
heavy (rain) **deras**
hell **neraka**
help (v) **bantu**
help, please **tolong**
herbs **rempah-rempah**
here **disini**
high **tinggi**
highway **jalan raya**
hiking **gerak jalan**
hill **bukit**
hire **séwa**
history **sejarah**
hitchhike **nunutan**
hobby **hobi**
hole **lubang**

holiday (v) **libur**
holiday (n) **liburan**
honest **jujur**
honey **madu**
honeymoon **bulan madu**
hope (v) **harap**
horrible **menakutkan**
horse **kuda**
hospital **rumah sakit**
hotel **hotél**
hour **jam**
house **rumah**
how **bagaimana**
how many **berapa banyak**
how much **berapa harga**
however **namun**
hug **peluk**
humid **lembab**
hundred **ratus**
hungry **lapar**
hunt, seek (v) **buru**
husband **suami**

**I**

I **saya, aku**
ice cream **és krim**
ice **és**
idea **idé**
identification (card) **(kartu) idéntitas**
if **kalau, jika**
ill, painful **sakit**
immigration **imigrasi**
important **penting**
included **termasuk**
infection **inféksi**
injection **suntik**
in-law (son-/daughter-) **menantu**
in-law (parents) **mertua**

inside **dalam**
insurance **asuransi**
interested **tertarik**
interesting **menarik**
Internet café **warnét**
Internet connection **konéksi Internét**
in the evening **pada malam hari**
in the morning **pada pagi hari**
invite **undang**
iron (for clothes) **setrika**
iron (v) **menyetrika**
island **pulau**
itchy **gatal**

**J**

jacket, coat **jas**
jackfruit **nangka**
Japan **Jepang**
jewelry **perhiasan**
job **pekerjaan**
journalist **wartawan, jurnalis**
journey **perjalanan**
juice **jus**
jump **lompat**

**K**

key **kunci**
kill (v) **bunuh**
killed **téwas**
kind **baik hati**
king **raja**
kiss **cium**
kitchen **dapur**
knife **pisau**
know **tahu**
know, meet **kenal**

# L

laces (for shoes) **tali sepatu**
ladder **tangga**
lake **danau**
lamp **lampu**
land (n) **tanah**
lane **gang**
language **bahasa**
large **besar**
last (endure) **makan waktu**
last (final) **terakhir**
late **terlambat, telat**
later **nanti**
laugh **tertawa**
launderette, laundry **binatu**
law **hukum**
lawyer **pengacara**
laxative **obat peluntur**
lazy **malas**
leaf **daun**
learn **belajar**
leather **kulit**
leather goods **kerajinan kulit**
leave, deposit **titip**
left (direction) **kiri**
lemon **jeruk nipis**
lend **pinjam**
leopard **macan**
less, fewer **kurang**
lesson **pelajaran**
library **perpustakaan**
lie (v) **bohong**
life **hidup**
light (n) **cahaya**
light (adj) **ringan**
lightning **kilat**
like (v) **suka**
line **garis**
lips **bibir**

list, menu **daftar**
listen **mendengarkan**
little (a little) **sedikit**
liver **hati**
long (time), old **lama**
look after **jaga**
lost (lost one's way) **tersesat**
lost (lost something) **hilang**
love **cinta**
lover, darling **kekasih**
lucky **untung**
lunch **makan siang**

# M

madam **ibu, nyonya**
machine **mesin**
magazine **majalah**
magic **sihir**
main road **jalan raya**
make an appointment **buat janji**
makeup **dandan**
mall **mal**
man, male **laki-laki, pria**
mango **manga**
manicure **manikur**
mankind **manusia**
many, lots **banyak**
map **péta**
marital status **status (perkawainan)**
market **pasar**
married **menikah**
mask **topeng**
massage **pijat**
matches **korék api**
matter, subject **hal**
mattress **kasur**
may (have permission) **boléh**

maybe **mungkin**
mayor **walikota**
meal **makanan**
mean (v) **berarti**
measure **ukur**
meat **daging**
mechanic's workshop
  **béngkél**
medicine **obat**
medium (size) **sedang**
meet **ke temu**
member **anggota**
menu **menu**
meter (in taxi) **argo**
midday **siang**
migraine **sakit kepala**
  **sebelah**
military, army **tentara**
milk **susu**
million **juta**
mineral water **air mineral**
minute **menit**
miss (flight, train)
  **ketinggalan**
missing person **orang hilang**
mistaken **keliru**
misunderstanding **salah**
  **paham**
mix **campur**
mobile phone **HP, ponsél**
moment **saat**
Monday **Senin**
money **uang**
moneychanger **penukaran**
  **uang**
monkey **monyét**
month **bulan**
more (more than) **lebih**
more **lagi**
morning **pagi**

mosque **mesjid**
mosquito **nyamuk**
mosquito net **kelambu**
mosquito repellent **obat**
  **nyamuk**
most **paling**
mother, Mrs. **ibu**
mother-in-law **ibu mertua**
motorbike **sepéda motor**
mountain **gunung**
mouse **tikus**
mouth **mulut**
move, change **pindah**
MSG **vetsin**
much **banyak**
mud **lumpur**
museum **musium**
mushroom, grow rapidly
  **jamur**
music **musik**
mutton **daging domba**

**N**
nail (finger) **kuku**
naked **telanjang, bugil**
name **nama**
nappy, diaper **popok**
nation **bangsa**
nature **alam**
natural **alami**
naughty **nakal**
nausea, to feel nauseous
  **mual**
near, nearby **dekat**
neck **leher**
need **perlu**
neighbor **tetangga**
nephew **keponakan**
net **jaring**
never **belum pernah**

new **baru**
news **berita, kabar**
newspaper **koran**
next (after that) **kemudian**
next to **sebelah**
nice (pleasant)
  **menyenangkan**
nice (person) **baik**
niece **keponakan**
night **malam**
nightclub **klub malam**
no **tidak, nggak, gak, tak**
noodles **mie**
normal, usual **biasa**
north **utara**
nose **hidung**
not **bukan**
not yet **belum**
note **nota**
notebook **buku catatan**
now **sekarang**
nowhere **tidak di**
  **mana-mana**
number **nomor**
nut **kacang**

## O

occupation **perkerjaan**
ocean **samudera**
office **kantor**
often **sering**
oil **minyak**
old **tua**
on the left **di sebelah kiri**
on the right **di sebelah**
  **kanan**
on the way **dalam**
  **perjalanan**
on time **tepat waktu**
onion **bawang**

only **hanya, saja, cuma**
open **buka**
opposite **lawan**
or **atau**
orange (colour) **oren**
orange (fruit) **(buah) jeruk**
order, reserve **pesan**
original **asli**
other **lain**
outside **luar**
overseas **luar negeri**
own (v) **milik**
owner **pemilik**

## P

pads (sanitary napkins)
  **pembalut**
page **halaman**
painkillers **penawar sakit**
paint (v) **lukis**
paint (n) **cat**
pajamas **piyama**
paper **kertas**
parents **orang tua**
park (v) **parkir**
park (n) **taman**
party (celebration) **pésta**
party (political) **partai**
passenger **penumpang**
passport **paspor**
past **masa lalu**
pay (v) **bayar**
people, populace **rakyat**
perfect **sempurna**
permit, permission **ijin**
period (menstruation;
  menses) **datang bulan**
person **orang**
petrol **bensin**
pharmacy **apotik**

pickpocket **copét**
pick up **mengambil**
picture **gambar**
pig **babi**
pillow **bantal**
pineapple **nanas**
place **tempat**
plain (not flavored) **tawar**
plan **rencana**
plate **piring**
play (v) **main**
playing cards **kartu remi**
pocket **kantong**
poison **racun**
police **polisi**
poor **miskin**
pork **daging babi**
possible **mungkin**
postage stamp **perangko**
postcode **kode pos**
postpone **tunda**
potato **kentang**
power outlet **stopkontak**
prawn **udang**
prayer **doa**
precious stone **batu mulia**
pregnant **hamil**
prescription **resep dokter**
pretty **cantik**
price **harga**
print (v) **cétak**
prison **penjara**
private **pribadi**
problem **masalah**
program **program**
promise **janji**
proud **bangga**
public **umum**
pull **tarik**
pull a muscle **keseleo**

punctured **bocor**
purple **ungu**
purse (wallet) **dompét**
push **dorong**

**Q**
quality **kwalitas**
queen **ratu**
question **pertanyaan**
queue (v) **antri**
quick **cepat**
quiet **sepi**

**R**
rabbit **kelinci**
rain **hujan**
rainbow **pelangi**
raincoat **jas hujan**
rarely **jarang**
raw **mentah**
razor **alat cukur**
read (v) **baca**
ready **siap**
really **sungguh**
receipt **kwitansi**
receive **terima**
recover **sembuh**
red **mérah**
red wine **(minuman) anggur mérah**
refrigerator **lemari és**
refund **uang kembali**
refuse, reject **tolak**
region, area **daérah**
relax **santai**
religion **agama**
remember **ingat**
remote **terpencil**
rent, hire (v) **séwa**
repeat **ulang**

reply **balas, jawab**
report (police) **laporan polisi**
resemble **mirip**
rest **istirahat**
restaurant **réstoran**
return, come back **kembali**
rice (cooked) **nasi**
rice (uncooked) **beras**
rich **kaya**
right (direction) **kanan**
ring **cincin**
ripe **matang**
river **sungai, kali**
road **jalan**
rob **rampok**
romantic **romantis**
roof **atap**
room **kamar**
room, space **ruang**
room service **layanan kamar**
rubber **karét**
rubbish, garbage **sampah**
rude **kurang ajar**
run (*v*) **lari**
running shoes **sepatu olahraga**

## S
sad **sedih**
safe **aman**
safe (*n*) **lemari bési**
sail (*v*) **berlayar**
salary **gaji**
sale **obral**
salt **garam**
same **sama**
sand **pasir**
Saturday **Sabtu**
say **bilang**
scared **takut**

schedule **jadwal**
school **sekolah**
science **ilmu**
scissors **gunting**
Scotland **Skotlandia**
scream **teriak**
scuba diving **selam**
sea **laut**
seafood **makanan laut**
seasick **mabuk laut**
search, look for **cari**
season **musim**
seat **kursi**
secret **rahasia**
see **lihat**
seed **biji**
sell **jual**
send **kirim**
sew **jahit**
sex **séks**
sexy **séksi**
shampoo **sampo**
shave **cukur**
shaver **alat cukur**
shaving cream **krem cukur**
sheep **domba**
ship **kapal**
shirt **keméja**
shocked **kaget**
shoe **sepatu**
shop (*n*) **toko**
shop (*v*), shopping **belanja**
short **péndék**
shorts (clothing) **celana péndék**
shrimp **udang**
shut up **diam**
shut **tutup**
shy, embarrassed **malu**
side **sisi**

sightseeing **wisata**
sign (road) **papan jalan**
signature **tanda tangan**
silence **kesunyian**
silk **sutra**
silver **pérak**
since **sejak**
sing **nyani**
single (only one) **satu**
single (unmarried) **belum menikah**
sir **bapak, tuan**
sister **saudara perempuan, adik (perempuran)**
sit **duduk**
size **ukuran**
skin, leather **kulit**
skirt **rok**
sky **langit**
sleep **tidur**
sleepy **mengantuk**
slippery **licin**
slow **pelan**
slowly **pelan-pelan**
small **kecil**
small change **uang kecil**
smell, smelly **bau**
smile **senyum**
smoke (cigarette) **merokok**
snail **kéong**
snake **ular**
snorkel **snorkél**
soap **sabun**
socks **kaos kaki**
soft **halus**
some **beberapa**
someone **ada orang**
something **sesuatu**
sometimes **kadang-kadang**
son **anak (laki-laki)**

song **lagu**
sore throat **sakit tenggorokan**
sorry **maaf**
soul **jiwa**
south **selatan**
souvenir **oléh-oléh, kenang-kenangan**
speak **bicara**
spicy **pedas**
spider **laba-laba**
split **belah**
spoilt **manja**
spoon **séndok**
sport **olahraga**
sprain **keseléo**
squid **cumi-cumi**
stairs **tangga**
star **bintang**
station (railway) **statsiun**
stay (overnight) **menginap**
stay **tinggal**
steal **curi**
still **masih**
stomach **perut**
stomach ache **sakit perut**
stone **batu**
stop (bus) **halte bis**
stop (v) **berhenti**
story **cerita**
straw (drinking) **sedotan**
strength **kuasa**
string **tali**
strong **kuat**
struggle **juang**
student (university) **mahasiswa**
stupid, idiot **bodoh**
sugar **gula**
suggestion **saran**

suitable **sesuai**
suitcase **kopor**
summer **musim panas**
sun **matahari**
Sunday **Hari Minggu**
sunglasses **kacamata hitam**
sunny **cerah**
surf (waves) **ombak**
surfboard **papan selancar**
surname **nama keluarga**
surprise **kejutan**
suspicious **curiga**
swap, change **tukar**
sweat **keringat**
sweater **baju hangat**
sweet **manis**
swim (v) **renang**
swimming pool **kolam renang**

**T**
table **méja**
tail **ékor**
take off, remove **lepas**
take **ambil**
talkative **ceréwét**
tall **tinggi**
tampons **tampon**
taste **rasa**
tax **pajak**
taxi **taksi**
tea **téh**
teacher **guru**
teenager **remaja, anak muda**
teeth **gigi**
telephone **télépon**
tempt **goda**
tennis **ténis**
thank you, thanks **terima kasih**

that **itu**
there **disana**
they **meréka**
thief **pencuri**
thief **maling**
thin **tipis**
think **pikir**
thirsty **haus**
this **ini**
this afternoon **siang ini**
this morning **pagi ini**
thorn, spike **duri**
throw away **buang**
thunder **guntur**
Thursday **Kamis**
ticket **tikét, karcis**
ticket counter **lokét**
ticklish **geli**
tie (v) **ikat**
tiger **harimau**
time, when (past) **waktu**
tire **ban**
tired **capék**
tissues **tisu**
today **hari ini**
together **bersama**
toilet **kamar kecil, WC**
toilet paper **kertas toilet**
toiletries **perlengkapan**
tomorrow **bésok**
tonight **nanti malam**
too **terlalu**
toothbrush **sikat gigi**
toothpaste **pasta gigi**
top **atas**
tourism **pariwisata**
tourist information office **kantor informasi wisata**
towel **handuk**
toy **mainan**

traffic **lalu lintas**
train (*n*) **keréta api**
train station **stasiun keréta api**
translate **terjemahkan**
traveler; tourist **turis, pelancong**
tree **pohon**
trick, cheat **tipu**
trouble, worry (*v*) **répot-répot**
trousers **celana**
true **benar**
trustworthy **terpercaya**
try (*v*) **coba**
Tuesday **Selasa**
turn (*v*) **bélok**
turn off **matikan**
turn on **pasang**
TV **tévé/télévisi**
twin bed **dua tempat tidur**
twins **kembar**

**U**
ugly, bad **jelék**
umbrella **payung**
underpants **celana dalam**
under **di bawah**
understand **paham, mengerti**
unemployed **mengaggur**
university **universitas**
unkind, mean **jahat**
until **sampai**
up **atas**
urinate **kencing**
use **pakai**
usually **biasanya**

**V**
vacant **kosong**
vacation **liburan**
vain **sombong**
various **anéka**
vegetable **sayur**
vegetarian **végétarian**
very **sekali, banget**
via **léwat**
view (*n*) **pandangan**
victim **korban**
villa **vila**
village **désa**
visit **kunjungan**
vitamins **vitamin**
voice **suara**
volcano **gunung api**
vomit **muntah**

**W**
wait (*v*) **tunggu**
walk (*v*) **jalan kaki**
wall **dinding**
wallet **dompét**
want (*v*) **mau, ingin**
war **perang**
warm **hangat**
wash (*v*) **cuci**
washing machine **mesin cuci**
wasteful **boros**
watch (*n*) **jam tangan**
watch (*v*) **nonton**
water **air**
water-skiing **ski air**
watersports **olahraga air**
wave (*n*) **ombak**
way (direction) **arah**
we **kita, kami**
weak **lemah**
wear **pakai**

weather **cuaca**
wedding **perkawinan**
Wednesday **Rabu**
week **minggu**
weekend **akhir pekan**
weigh **timbang**
weird **anéh**
west **barat**
wet **basah**
what **apa**
what's more **apalagi**
whatever, moreover **apa saja**
wheel **roda**
when **kapan**
whenever **kapan saja**
while **sambil**
which one **mana**
whisky **wiski**
white **putih**
who **siapa**
why **kenapa**
wide **luas, lébar**
widow **janda**
widower **duda**
wife **istri**
wild **liar**
will (future) **akan**
wind **angin**

window **jendéla**
wine **anggur**
with **dengan, sama**
without **tanpa**
woman **perempuan, wanita**
wood **kayu**
wool **wol**
word, say **kata**
work (v) **kerja**
world **dunia**
worry (v) **khwatir**
wound **luka**
wrap **bungkus**
wrist **pergelangan tangan**
write **tulis**
wrong **salah**

**Y**
year **tahun**
yellow **kuning**
yes **ya**
yesterday **kemarin**
you **anda, kamu**
you're welcome **sama-sama**

**Z**
zip **kancing tarik**
zoo **kebun binatang**

## ABOUT TUTTLE
## "Books to Span the East and West"

Our core mission at Tuttle Publishing is to create books which bring people together one page at a time. Tuttle was founded in 1832 in the small New England town of Rutland, Vermont (USA). Our fundamental values remain as strong today as they were then—to publish best-in-class books informing the English-speaking world about the countries and peoples of Asia. The world has become a smaller place today and Asia's economic, cultural and political influence has expanded, yet the need for meaningful dialogue and information about this diverse region has never been greater. Since 1948, Tuttle has been a leader in publishing books on the cultures, arts, cuisines, languages and literatures of Asia. Our authors and photographers have won numerous awards and Tuttle has published thousands of books on subjects ranging from martial arts to paper crafts. We welcome you to explore the wealth of information available on Asia at **www.tuttlepublishing.com**.

Published by Tuttle Publishing, an imprint of Periplus Editions (HK) Ltd.

**www.tuttlepublishing.com**

Copyright © 2017 Periplus Editions (HK) Ltd.
All rights reserved.

**Distributed by**

**Indonesia**
PT Java Books Indonesia
Kawasan Industri Pulogadung, Jl. Rawa Gelam
IV No. 9, Jakarta 13930, Indonesia
Tel: (62) 21 4682 1088
Fax: (62) 21 461 0206
crm@periplus.co.id
www.periplus.com

**Japan**
Tuttle Publishing
Yaekari Building 3F, 5-4-12 Osaki,
Shinagawa-ku, Tokyo 141-0032, Japan
Tel: (81) 3 5437 0171
Fax: (81) 3 5437 0755
sales@tuttle.co.jp
www.tuttle.co.jp

**North America, Latin America & Europe**
Tuttle Publishing
364 Innovation Drive
North Clarendon, VT 05759-9436, USA
Tel: 1 (802) 773 8930
Fax: 1 (802) 773 6993
info@tuttlepublishing.com
www.tuttlepublishing.com

**Asia-Pacific**
Berkeley Books Pte Ltd
61 Tai Seng Avenue #02-12,
Singapore 534167
Tel: (65) 6280 1330
Fax: (65) 6280 6290
Email: inquiries@periplus.com.sg
www.periplus.com

Library of Congress Control Number: 2017956491
ISBN 978-0-8048-4691-2

20 19 18     5 4 3 2 1     1711MP     Printed in Singapore

TUTTLE PUBLISHING® is a registered trademark of Tuttle Publishing,
a division of Periplus Editions (HK) Ltd.